Counselor Education for the Twenty-First Century

Critical Studies in Education and Culture Series

Counselor Education for the Twenty-First Century

Susan J. Brotherton

Critical Studies in Education and Culture Series
Edited by Henry A. Giroux and Paulo Freire

BERGIN & GARVEY
Westport, Connecticut • London

Library of Congress Cataloging-in-Publication Data

Brotherton, Susan J.
   Counselor education for the twenty-first century / Susan J.
   Brotherton.
      p.   cm.—(Critical studies in education and culture series,
   ISSN 1064–8615)
      Includes bibliographical references and index.
      ISBN 0–89789–471–5 (alk. paper)
      1. Student counselors—Training of—United States.   2. Critical
   pedagogy—United States.   I. Title.   II. Series.
   LB1731.75.B76   1996
   371.2′022—dc20   95–39389

British Library Cataloguing in Publication Data is available.

Library of Congress Catalog Card Number: 95–39389
ISBN: 0–89789–471–5
ISSN: 1064–8615

First published in 1996

Bergin & Garvey, 88 Post Road West, Westport, CT 06881
An imprint of Greenwood Publishing Group, Inc.

Printed in the United States of America

The paper used in this book complies with the
Permanent Paper Standard issued by the National
Information Standards Organization (Z39.48–1984).

10 9 8 7 6 5 4 3 2 1

Copyright Acknowledgments

The author and publisher gratefully acknowledge permission to use the following:

Excerpts from Antonia Darder, *Culture and Power in the Classroom*. 1991. Westport, CT: Bergin &
Garvey. Reprinted with permission of Greenwood Publishing Group, Inc., Westport, CT. Copyright
© 1991 by Antonia Darder.

Excerpts from William G. Tierney, *Building Communities of Difference*. 1993. Westport, CT: Bergin
& Garvey. Reprinted with permission of Greenwood Publishing Group, Inc., Westport, CT. Copyright © 1993 by William G. Tierney.

Excerpts from Edmund V. Sullivan, *Critical Psychology and Pedagogy*. 1990. Westport, CT: Bergin
& Garvey. Reprinted with permission of Greenwood Publishing Group, Inc., Westport, CT. Copyright © 1990 by Bergin & Garvey.

Copyright © 1991, by the Regents of the University of Minnesota. Reprinted from *Postmodern Education: Politics, Culture, and Social Criticism*, by S. Aronowitz and H. A. Giroux, published by the
University of Minnesota Press.

To my sister, Anne L. Brotherton—
who in her life knew oppression
and now knows freedom—let your spirit soar;
and to my trusted confidant, friend, and critic,
Sheila A. Williams.

Understanding one another's pain and one another's views of the world and community are essential for academic institutions [counselors] as we approach the next century. Education concerns the ability of people to come to terms with their own and others' identities, and to understand how the world shapes and is shaped by social interaction. And such knowledge is not merely to be learned for learning's sake; rather, it is to be employed in the work of building democracy—in our organizations, in our communities, and in our nation.

William Tierney
Building Communities of Difference

Contents

Series Foreword

Within the last decade, the debate over the meaning and purpose of education has occupied the center of political and social life in the United States. Dominated largely by an aggressive and ongoing attempt by various sectors of the Right, including "fundamentalists," nationalists, and political conservatives, the debate over educational policy has been organized around a set of values and practices that take as their paradigmatic model the laws and ideology of the marketplace and the imperatives of a newly emerging cultural traditionalism. In the first instance, schooling is being redefined through a corporate ideology that stresses the primacy of choice over community, competition over cooperation, and excellence over equity. At stake here is the imperative to organize public schooling around the related practices of competition, reprivatization, standardization, and individualism.

In the second instance, the New Right has waged a cultural war against schools as part of a wider attempt to contest the emergence of new public cultures and social movements that have begun to demand that schools take seriously the imperatives of living in a multiracial and multicultural democracy. The contours of this cultural offensive are evident in the call by the Right for standardized testing, the rejection of multiculturalism, and the development of curricula around what is euphemistically called a "common culture." In this perspective, the notion of a common culture serves as a referent to denounce any attempt by subordinate groups to challenge the narrow ideological and political parameters by which such a culture both defines and expresses itself. It is not too surprising that the theoretical and political distance between defining schools around a common culture and denouncing cultural difference as the enemy of democratic life is relatively short indeed.

This debate is important not simply because it makes visible the role that schools play as sites of political and cultural contestation, but because it is within this debate that the notion of the United States as an open and democratic society is being questioned and redefined. Moreover, this debate provides a challenge to progressive educators both in and outside of the United States to address a number of conditions central to a postmodern world. First, public schools cannot be seen as either objective or neutral. As institutions actively involved in constructing political subjects and presupposing a vision of the future, they must be dealt with in terms that are simultaneously historical, critical, and transformative. Second, the relationship between knowledge and power in schools places undue emphasis on disciplinary structures and on individual achievement as the primary unit of value. Critical educators need a language that emphasizes how social identities are constructed within unequal relations of power in the schools and how schooling can be organized through interdisciplinary approaches to learning and cultural differences that address the dialectical and multifaceted experiences of everyday life. Third, the existing cultural transformation of American society into a multiracial and multicultural society structured in multiple relations of domination demands that we address how schooling can become sites for cultural democracy rather than channeling colonies reproducing new forms of nativism and racism. Finally, critical educators need a new language that takes seriously the relationship between democracy and the establishment of those teaching and learning conditions that enable forms of self and social determination in students and teachers. This suggest not only new forms of self-definition for human agency, it also points to redistributing power within the school and between the school and the larger society.

Critical Studies in Education and Culture is intended as both a critique and as a positive response to these concerns and the debates from which they emerge. Each volume is intended to address the meaning of schooling as a form of cultural politics and cultural work as a pedagogical practice that serves to deepen and extend the possibilities of democratic public life. Broadly conceived, some central considerations present themselves as defining concerns of the Series. Within the last decade, a number of new theoretical discourse and vocabularies have emerged that challenge the narrow disciplinary boundaries and theoretical parameters that construct the traditional relationship among knowledge, power, and schooling. The emerging discourses of feminism, post-colonialism, literary studies, cultural studies, and post-modernism have broadened our understanding of how schools work as sites of containment and possibility. No longer content to view schools as objective institutions engaged in the transmission of an unproblematic cultural heritage, the new discourses illuminate how schools function as cultural sites actively engaged in the production of not only knowledge but social identities. *Critical Studies in Education and Culture* will attempt to encourage this type of analysis by emphasizing how schools might be addressed as border institutions or sites of crossing actively involved in exploring, reworking, and translating the ways in which culture is produced, negotiated, and rewritten.

Emphasizing the centrality of politics, culture, and power, *Critical Studies in Education and Culture* will deal with pedagogical issues that contribute in novel ways to our understanding of how critical knowledge, democratic values, and social practices can provide a basis for teachers, students, and other cultural workers to redefine their role as engaged and public intellectuals.

As part of a broader attempt to rewrite and refigure the relationship between education and culture, *Critical Studies in Education and Culture* is interested in work that is interdisciplinary, critical, and addresses the emergent discourses on gender, race, sexual preference, class, ethnicity, and technology. In this respect, the Series is dedicated to opening up new discursive and public spaces for critical interventions into schools and other pedagogical sites. To accomplish this, each volume will attempt to rethink the relationship between language and experience, pedagogy and human agency, and ethics and social responsibility as part of a larger project for engaging and deepening the prospects of democratic schooling in a multiracial and multicultural society. Concerns central to this Series include addressing the political economy and deconstruction of visual, aural, and printed texts, issues of difference and multiculturalism, relationships between language and power, pedagogy as a form of cultural politics, and historical memory and the construction of identity and subjectivity.

Critical Studies in Education and Culture is dedicated to publishing studies that move beyond the boundaries of traditional and existing critical discourses. It is concerned with making public schooling a central expression of democratic culture. In doing so it emphasizes works that combine cultural politics, pedagogical criticism, and social analyses with self-reflective tactics that challenge and transform those configurations of power that characterize the existing system of education and other public cultures.

Henry A. Giroux

Preface

Counselors often are called "change agents." This label is used as a description of the impact a counselor may have on an individual or family. For there to be equality in our multifaceted society, counselors must become change agents in a wider sphere. They are the ones to bring about counselor training reform, equality of mental health services, and personal commitments to more than the multicultural counseling issues outlined here. A change in curricula or techniques is not enough as long as there fails to be a critique of the larger social order and a plan of action for transformation. The optimum goals of education and educational counseling should be liberation, creating the foundation for equality, empowerment, social justice, and a qualitatively better life for all. Counselors must have the intellectual, emotional, and spiritual ability to critically question the social impact of their practice and, further, critically question the oppressive nature of the theoretical foundation that supports their practice.

This book examines the need and developmental support of an expanded theoretical foundation of counselor education that will serve to better prepare school counselors for effectively meeting student counseling needs in the twenty-first century. This process includes a rethinking of meanings and outcomes associated with counselor education, the counseling process, the role of the school counselor, and the political implications embedded in educational counseling. The ultimate goal of this book is to offer the field of counselor education a theoretical foundation that produces a shift in the dimensionality of school counselor education and preparation.

The necessity for an expanded theoretical framework will be substantiated by: (1) questioning the applicability and relevance to practice of current counselor education; (2) critically analyzing traditional psychological philosophy; (3) investigating the principles behind critical theory, feminist theory, and postmodernism; (4) unveiling the exclusionary aspects of current counseling theory and practice; (5) examining a proposed paradigm shift in counselor education, that of critical postmodernism; and (6) presenting two classroom applications of a critical postmodern approach to counselor education.

The theoretical impetus for this project can be found in the works of the postmodernists, Stanley Aronowitz, Henry Giroux, and William Tierney; the critical theorists, Peter McLaren and Antonio Gramsci; the critical pedagogists, Paulo Freire and Antonia Darder; and the critical psychologist, Edmund Sullivan.

Our journey into counselor education for the twenty-first century begins with the identification and exploration of the current pedagogical shift that was brought about by the growing cultural diversity in the United States. It is here in Chapter 1, that we begin to discover a monocultural resistance to progress, change, and advancement of justice within members of the profession. Next, by taking a deeper look at the exclusionary aspects of the psychological foundations of counselor education in Chapter 2, one begins to unmask previously unquestioned power structures and biases embedded in counselor education. Then, through the introduction of critical theory, Chapter 3; an exploration of critical pedagogy and educational counseling, Chapter 4; aspects of critical psychology, Chapter 5; and the impact of the economic, social, and political times in which we live, Chapter 6, we discover some important shifts needed in the theoretical dimensions of counselor education. The central themes of this theoretical shift are *inclusion* as opposed to exclusion, *fluidity* as opposed to rigid notions, *diversity* as opposed to ethnocentrism, and *relational realities* as opposed to universal truths. Lastly, along this journey, we shall begin to imagine how these expanded theoretical foundations might look when applied to a classroom setting. Chapter 7 describes a pilot project whereby the theoretical foundation proposed in this book was incorporated in an introductory course in counseling. A critical postmodern approach to a multicultural counseling course is discussed in Chapter 8. Again, our travel into the next century begins with the multicultural counseling movement.

As counselor educators face the challenges of preparing professional counselors to promote equality and justice in American schools in the next century, issues surrounding diversity, multiplicity, and exclusion must be addressed fervently. No longer can ethnocentric, encapsulated, and exclusionary aspects of counselor education be tolerated. The primary purpose of this book is to voice theoretical principles from which a critical postmodern pedagogy may be developed. It is an attempt to provide a path for the crossing over, not out, of differences and to establish an element of fluidity in counseling theory and practice. In essence, it sets forth a pedagogy of inclusion that allows for the honoring of difference and the advancement of social justice.

Acknowledgments

I extend my deepest appreciation to the many friends, teachers, colleagues, and students who have encouraged and helped me during the preparation of this work. My special thanks to Antonia Darder, my mentor and teacher, whose courage, spirit, and intellectual position challenged me to "stay at the table" when resistance and discomfort were served, and whose life has empowered, enriched, and changed mine—I thank you for having faith and confidence in my ability; to Daryl Smith, my advisor, teacher, and friend, who never let me leave her office without first having me explore some connection between my intellectual, emotional, spiritual, and personal lives; to my associates at California State University, San Bernardino, for the professional and personal support given; to Nancy Kimbrough and Cari Card for their "hawk eyes" and editing assistance; to my dear friend, Karen Yoshino, for her ever-constant friendship, love, interest, and intellectual challenge; and to Sheila A. Williams, for all of the times we have struggled together for understanding, and for crossing this finish line with me.

1

Multiculturalism: Forcing a Change in Counselor Education

Although counseling has traditionally emphasized the importance of freedom, rational thought, tolerance, equality, and justice, it has also been used as an oppressive instrument by those in power to maintain the status quo. Whenever counseling is used to restrict rather than foster the well-being and development of culturally different persons, then counselors are participating in overt or covert forms of prejudice and discrimination.

Paul B. Pedersen
"Multiculturalism as a Generic Approach to Counseling"
Journal of Counseling and Development

The United States is undergoing an unprecedented demographic transformation. It is predicted that, by the year 2000, the beginning of the twenty-first century, the majority of the people living in the United States will be individuals from diverse cultural, ethnic, and racial groups. This, coupled with the economic, social, political, and global changes taking place at a breathtaking pace, has forced the onset of a shift in the ideology that informs educational counseling. Leading scholars in the field encourage a more developmental perspective to counseling. This means that counselors need to understand their clients' developmental histories in order to counsel effectively (Van Hesteren & Ivey, 1990).

The cultural shifts taking place in the United States dictate the need for counselors to become culturally competent (Atkinson, Morten, & Sue, 1983; Henderson, 1979; LeVine & Padilla, 1980; Pederson, Draguns, Lonner, & Trimble, 1981; Sue, 1981). Multicultural training in counselor education programs, however, is a recent innovation that is not widespread (Ibrahim & Thompson, 1982; Ponterotto & Casas, 1987). Although emphasis on multicultural training in counselor education programs is most likely to increase

(Heath, Neimeyer, & Frye, 1988), most current school counselors lack adequate and systematic training in multicultural counseling.

The emergence and increase of cross-cultural counseling offerings in counselor education seem to be responses to several factors. One important factor is the growing recognition that traditional counseling approaches have failed to meet the needs of cultural and ethnic minorities (Ponterotto & Casas, 1987; Sue & Sue, 1990). A second factor is the emerging consideration and encouragement of multicultural variables in core curricula by program accreditation standards, such as those of the Council for Accreditation of Counseling and Related Educational Programs (CACREP), the American Psychological Association (APA), and the National Counsel for the Accreditation for Teacher Education (NCATE). A third factor is the growing recognition of the increasingly multicultural nature of the populations served by mental health professionals. Approximately 15.7 percent of the population of the United States is composed of people whose racial/ethnic background is something other than white (United States Bureau of the Census, 1990); and it is estimated that by the turn of the century, one-third of the United States' population will be Spanish speaking. The United States Census Bureau (1990) estimates that the largest growing racial group, raising from 9 million in 1992—3 percent of the population—to 41 million in 2050—11 percent of the population—is that of Asian and Pacific Islanders. In certain regions of the United States and within particular states, including California, there are concentrated pockets of diverse races and cultures. Therefore, some communities and schools have subsequently high proportions of bicultural populations. These changing demographics add to the many new challenges faced by counselors and counselor educators.

As was mentioned previously, there is an increasing recognition within the professional ranks that the existing psychological and counseling training paradigm simply does not accurately or adequately address the mental health needs of people from different cultural backgrounds and other special populations (Atkinson, Morten, & Sue, 1989). The multicultural counseling movement has emerged as a response to such a deprived reality. This movement in counselor education will ensure as potent and encompassing an influence as the client-centered movement of the 1950s and 1960s.

Multiculturalism has been labeled the most important new idea to shape the field of counseling in the past 20 years. According to Paul Pedersen (1991), "we are moving toward a generic theory of multiculturalism as a 'fourth force' position, complementary to the other three forces of psychodynamic, behavior, and humanistic explanations of human behavior" (p. 6). The description of multiculturalism as a fourth force has grown from research that focuses on multicultural counseling as a process (Pedersen, 1988, 1990; Ponterotto & Casas, 1987; Sue & Sue, 1990). The designation of a fourth force emphasizes that multiculturalism is relevant throughout the field of counseling as a generic rather than an exotic perspective. Labels tend to oversimplify complicated relationships, and to that extent they are dangerous. This label, however, deliberately calls attention to the way in which a *multicultural* perspective has changed the way we look at counseling across fields and at theories. Multiculturalism has become recognized as a powerful force that is essential for understanding persons of color, and also for comprehending ourselves and our interrelationships in a complicated social context.

There exists some debate over the scope of the use and function of the term multiculturalism. Some counselor educators believe that the term should be used to separate and identify differences according to race and ethnicity only (Lee & Richardson, 1991; Locke, 1990). They argue against broadening the definition of culture because there is the danger of diffusing the term to a point of insignificance. Therefore, they contend that courses taught in multicultural counseling should focus on this fairly narrow definition of multiculturalism. Still others (Fukuyama, 1990) believe that additional groups, such as the disabled, gays and lesbians, Jews, and others, should be identified in a cultural context.

In reality, it can be said that all counseling is cross-cultural. According to Pedersen (1994), "By defining *culture* broadly, to include demographic variables (e.g., age, gender, place of residence), status variables (e.g., social, educational, economic), and affiliations (formal and informal), as well as ethnographic variables such as nationality, ethnicity, language, and religion, the construct of 'multicultural' becomes generic to all counseling relationships" (p. 16). Additionally, variables dealing with sexual orientation and family structure, along with abilities and disabilities, should be inclusive in the definition and discussion of culture. Using the broader definition of culture provides a framework for integrating same and/or different behaviors, emotions, and expectations within changing contexts.

The multicultural perspective seeks to provide a conceptual framework that recognizes the complex diversity of a composite society while simultaneously suggesting bridges of shared concern that bind together culturally different persons. The ultimate outcome may be a multicultural theory or, as offered as the purpose of this book, a theoretical paradigm shift that attempts to meet the needs of the future. As some scholars suggest (Segall, Dansan, Berry, & Poortinga, 1990), "there may well come a time when we will no longer speak of cross-cultural psychology as such. The basic premise of this field—that to understand human behavior, we must study it in its sociocultural context—may become so widely accepted that all psychology will be inherently cultural" (p. 352). A recent survey of American School Counselors Association (ASCA) members found a strong expression of the need for multicultural education from the counselors responding to the survey (Carey, Reinat, & Fontes, 1990). Clearly, school counselors recognize the need for a broad understanding of multicultural issues and counseling skills in order to be effective in today's educational settings. With the gradual demographic shifts that have been taking place for the last two decades, it seems inconceivable that counselor education programs have yet to systematically integrate multiculturalism and diversity in their curricula. This fact is but another indicator of the monocultural, ethnocentric nature of such programs.

HISTORY OF MULTICULTURAL COUNSELING EDUCATION

Psychology and counseling have not earned admirable records in educating students or faculty members about the importance of socioenvironmental factors. In particular, the roles of race, ethnicity, and gender forces in behavior have received less than adequate attention (Albee, 1981). Emphatically stated, Albee (1981) posited that the history of prejudice, which long has been part of the teaching by psychologists, is the cause for shame and repentance. There is, therefore, an urgent need for psychology and counseling instructional programs to retool and prepare themselves and students for our increasingly diverse and changing world.

Counselor training and practice long have been described as culturally encapsulated (Wrenn, 1962). In a stimulating review of the multicultural field (Parham, 1990), it was pointed out that the cultural limitations of helping have been part of African American writings for years. Leading scholars in the field have provided useful critiques which have assisted professional counselors in increasing their cultural awareness (Jackson, 1975; Pedersen, 1988; Sue, 1981). However, awareness alone is not enough, and systematic frameworks for teaching effective cross-cultural counseling skills are still in their infancy.

Most prominent theories of counseling originate from the Euro–North American cultural frame of individualistic–autonomous decision making, with a linear cause–effect view of the world. "Multicultural and cross-cultural approaches often seek to adapt existing Euro–North American theories and methods to new cultural frames. The problem with adaptation of existing methods is that they begin with traditional theoretical assumptions, which are culturally biased" (Nwachuku & Ivey, 1991, p. 106).

Although a historical overview of the multicultural counseling movement reflects a distinct pattern of progress in addressing the dire need for improved training practices, much work and improvement remain. There is currently no official public policy that uniformly governs, regulates, or mandates individual training program practices concerning multicultural counseling competencies; however, a variety of recommendations are offered by professional organizations. Consequently, institutional training practices vary greatly, as do the preparedness and skill level of new counselors.

CULTURAL ENCAPSULATION AND RACISM

If racism is defined as any program or practice of racial domination (Guralnik, 1976), one might reasonably argue that the counseling profession has perpetuated, and in many ways continues to perpetuate, this social dynamic.

Significant evidence exists to support this rather unpleasant proposition (D'Andrea & Daniels 1991).

First, from a numerical perspective, it is generally acknowledged that most minority groups are underrepresented in conventional counseling programs (Atkinson, Morton, & Sue, 1989). This underrepresentation is revealed by the minimal number of minority chairpersons, faculty, and students in counseling departments in this country. In fact, recent research suggests that the "trend toward minority underrepresentation among Hispanics, Blacks, and Asian Americans is more serious today than it was 6 years ago" (Young, Chamley, & Withers, 1990, p. 152). It also must be noted that, although many counseling programs reflect a disproportionate number of white, middle-class persons constituting the student body, an even greater disparity exists between the number of white men holding faculty and chairperson positions and that of women and minorities.

This sort of institutional arrangement reflects a type of racial and gender domination that, at the very least, unwittingly perpetuates cultural encapsulation within the profession. According to Micheal D'Andrea and Judy Daniels (1991),

Although not widely discussed, the obvious gap between the number of students-in-training who are neither white nor men, the increasing number of clients from diverse cultural-racial and socioeconomic backgrounds, and the preponderance of White, middle-class male counselor educators and administrators represents a scenario in which numerous ethical and moral questions might be raised. This situation becomes even more poignant when counselor educators and administrators are generally lacking in terms of their own level of multicultural counseling awareness, knowledge, and skills. (p. 78)

Second, ethnic and racial minorities have been identified as being clearly underserved and/or inappropriately served by the mental health system in the past (Special Populations Task Force of the President's Commission on Mental Health, 1978). Substandard treatment was found to be commonplace (Yamamoto, James, & Palley, 1968) and accompanied by negative psychological diagnoses (Lee & Temerlin, 1968). More recently, researchers have noted that the trend of inferior and differential counseling services continues for clients of differing racial and ethnic backgrounds (Abramowitz & Murray, 1983; White, 1984).

Third, the underutilization of mental health services by culturally diverse persons is, in part, due to the lack of minority counselors (Brown & Minor, 1990). Some experts suggest that minority group dissatisfaction with counseling reflects a general disillusionment with all of the social sciences due to the sheer lack of attention and emphasis on social injustices and problems encountered by minorities. In a somewhat similar perspective, Derald Wing Sue (1973) and Elsie Smith (1985) emphasized that the underrepresentation of minority groups in professional counseling training programs reinforces the perception that counseling is generally irrelevant to their needs.

Fourth, an important recurring theme appears in the professional literature that describes the discomfort of white counselors who find themselves working with persons from different cultural and/or racial populations (Margolis & Rungta, 1986). This discomfort is frequently rooted in negative stereotyping, lack of knowledge about the group of which the client is a member, or a generalized anxiety about working with different client populations. These conditions contribute to the provision of ineffective treatment by many counseling practitioners (Margolis & Rungta, 1986). In order to improve the mental health services utilized by persons of color, counselors must overcome their inadequacies concerning counseling persons different than themselves. Proponents of multiculturalism emphasize the need for major reform in counselor education programs and policies which could assist in the achievement of social justice for all persons (Brown & Minor, 1990).

MULTICULTURAL COUNSELOR EDUCATION MODELS

In recent years, serious questions have been raised about whether counselor education, as it is generally structured, enables students to grow in cross-cultural awareness and understanding (Lloyd, 1987). The theories and practice competencies to which students of counseling are exposed remain essentially monocultural (Katz, 1985). Research in the area of cross-cultural awareness development has been hampered by the lack of conceptual models that lend themselves to research in the context of diversity (Casas, 1985).

Theoretical counseling models taught in counselor education training programs imply that psychosocial development is uniform for all members of society, regardless of cultural or racial background. In these models, sociopolitical factors such as socioeconomics, class, and power are largely ignored, whereas selected variables of the authors' culture, such as individualism, are emphasized. Such models are of limited applicability in pluralistic societies (Katz, 1985).

Among the consequences of exclusive adherence to contemporary, white, Western cultural counseling theories and models are: (a) there has been a tendency to assume that psychosocial development occurs in a similarly orderly and uninterrupted progression for all; (b) ethnic and racial awareness and identity have not been considered noteworthy or integral aspects of the psychosocial development process; (c) cultural biases and taboos of a given author's society, including those relating to racism, prejudice, and discrimination, have been, albeit unwittingly, built into the model and its underlying theoretical assumptions; (d) members of society who do not represent the dominant culture find that the models do not "fit" their life experiences, either in whole or in part; (e) theories of deviance, deprivation, disadvantage, and abnormality have ensued, based on the extent to which the life experiences of various groups differ from the models proposed (Casas, 1985); and (f) research and interpretation have incorporated the biases and blind spots inherent in monocultural theoretical models.

In societies in which identifiable characteristics, such as immutable physical traits, become associated with the ascribed social status, a need to recognize the effect on the individual's psychosocial development exists (Smith, 1985). The process by which an individual becomes aware of being classified as a member of a high-status or low-status group, as well as the effect of this process and awareness on racial and ethnic minorities, began to receive attention during the 1970s, following the Civil Rights movement in the United States. Several authors have presented models dealing with the psychosocial development of minority groups. These models differ from earlier models by incorporating aspects of racial, ethnic, and cultural awareness as well as sociopolitical factors. Most deal with the development of the minority individual's awareness of ethnicity, or race consciousness, in their quest for self-identity. The three major approaches are minority typologies, developmental, and oppression as a common experience. The first two, typologies and developmental approaches, are traditional terms and approaches in counselor education.

The third approach is oppression as a common experience. This tends to be a very uncomfortable and, some believe, "radical" framework. This is true since to identify individuals as "oppressed" inherently means that there exists a dominant force. As this is concluded, we are forced to look at our own participation in the dominant–subordinate process, which serves to be disconcerting, to say the least. Since the more traditional approaches to minority developmental issues are more palatable by those in power, they are stressed in training programs. Consequently, the theory of oppressive experience is much less familiar to counselors, both cognitively and experimentally. This approach will be discussed briefly in terms of its value to improved counselor training.

Oppression, as a common experience, is the most recent approach to minority psychosocial development. This schema perceives the experiences of oppression as common to several identifiable groups, such as Asians, Latinos, blacks, and Aboriginal peoples. Atkinson, Morten, and Sue (1983) described five stages that oppressed people may experience in their "struggle to understand themselves in terms of their own minority culture, the dominant culture, and the oppressive relationship between the two" (p. 35): conformity, dissonance, resistance and immersion, introspection, and synergistic articulation and awareness. These stages are conceptualized as a continuous process.

Given the number of models that consider aspects of racial, ethnic, and cultural awareness as part of the psychosocial development of minority populations, there have been few attempts to conceptualize and document how representatives of the dominant culture acquire and alter their view of themselves and of minority groups (White & Sedlacek, 1987). Social justice cannot be realized in counseling, or in any other sphere, until dominant societies recognize and take responsibility for the immense creation and perpetuation of oppression among marginalized groups.

In 1979, a report by the Educational and Training Committee of Division 17, Counseling, of the APA (Sue et al., 1982) identified minimal cross-cultural competencies for training counselors. This paper outlined three areas of competencies of the culturally skilled counseling psychologist (p. 49). Cross-cultural training models emphasize one or more of the three competencies. The first area, or competency, concerns beliefs and attitudes, and requires that the counselor be culturally aware, in touch with his or her own biases about minority clients, comfortable with such differences, and sensitive to circumstances that may require the referral of minority clients to a same-culture counselor. The Cross-Cultural Dyadic Encounter (CCDE) (Beale, 1986) is one example of a training model that focuses on increasing cultural awareness. It is a "how-to" approach for counselors to increase understanding of backgrounds, values, and life-styles of clients from different cultures. This training exercise is designed to create an open dialogue between members from different ethnic groups and to deepen the appreciation and sensitivity of persons from these groups. The activity includes a series of open-ended questions and statements that elicit discussion and disclosure by the participants. While open exploration and discussion is extremely valuable in this endeavor, given the fact that the majority of counselor trainees are white, there may well be little variance in cultural backgrounds represented in these "open discussions." This may quickly lead to the continuance of stereotypical assumptions under the guise of increased counselor awareness and sensitivity.

The second competency area consists of command of knowledge, such as information sets, that the culturally skilled counseling psychologist should have. This knowledge should include an understanding of the effects that the sociopolitical system within the United States has on oppressed persons, culture-specific knowledge about the particular group being counseled, an understanding of the generic characteristics of counseling and psychotherapy, and knowledge of institutional barriers to the use of mental health services by nondominant groups. An example of a training model that attempts to address this type of skill development is the Ethnic Student Training Group program (Parker, Bingham, & Fukuyama, 1985). Student activities incorporated into this model include the intercultural interaction of unique and positive qualities of different cultures, case presentations of problems; techniques and strategies for working with ethnic students; panel presentations to help members gain knowledge of specific minority groups; a focus on concerns such as value changes, acculturation, generational differences, parental pressures, dating, and religious issues; and trainee case presentations for immediate supervision. What is missing from this model is the inclusion of activities dealing with intercultural tensions, internalized oppression, and the identification and meanings of resistance.

The third competency area concerns counseling skills. The culturally skilled counselor should have a wide repertoire of verbal and nonverbal responses, the ability to send messages accurately and appropriately, and the ability to use appropriate institutional intervention. Pedersen's (1988) Triad Model serves as an example of such training. The training program consists of simulated cross-cultural microcounseling interviews. The roleplays consist of a counselor, a client, and a pro-counselor (a supportive ally) or an anti-counselor (an antagonistic operator). The pro-counselor or anti-counselor acts as an internal dialogue of the counselor and the client to highlight salient cross-cultural issues that may affect the interaction between the two.

In order to effectively model and teach the above concepts and skills, the facilitating instructor must have the cultural, clinical, and supervisory expertise required; yet, most counselor educators are desperately lacking in multicultural awareness, knowledge, and skills. In addition, one may question the authenticity of the culture-specific information being used in the teaching activities.

A controversial issue in the training of cross-cultural counseling skills is whether to assume a universalist approach or a culture-specific approach. This controversy is well illustrated by the recent point–counterpoint section of *Counselor Education and Supervision* (Fukuyama, 1990). In this debate, Fukuyama took the universal or transcultural approach to cross-cultural counseling training. She proposed the universal approach for counseling interactions, pointing out the universal processes that go beyond cultural variations and by the commonalties shared by all minority groups.

On the other hand, Locke (1990) argued for cross-cultural counseling that emphasizes unique cultural group membership characteristics: the culture-specific approach. This approach asserts that the distinction between cultural and individual differences should be affirmed with each area addressed appropriately but separately. A person should be seen as an individual and as a member of his or her own cultural group. Locke (1990) introduced the importance of individual differences within a person's culture in the context of the dominant culture. Each culture is both dynamic and subjective, and his training stresses "learning to work in different cultures rather than merely learning about cultures" (p. 18). Although this approach moves toward the identification and validation of cultural uniqueness, it seems impossible to separate cultural and individual differences. In a bicultural society, one is always influenced by more than one culture.

Some recent training models have been more comprehensive in attempting to cover all three areas of cross-cultural counseling competencies as outlined in the APA Division 17 position paper (Sue et al., 1982). The majority of the programs, however, provide limited training opportunities for counselors. Not only are comprehensive cross-cultural training programs rare, but those that do exist provide only a partial solution.

CONSEQUENCES OF MULTICULTURAL COUNSELOR TRAINING MODELS

Counselors trained from the Euro–North American cultural belief system value self-disclosive, highly verbal, and goal-oriented clients. Total and immediate transparency is uncommon among clients of any ethnicity, and the clients' right to withhold their most private thoughts, feelings, and behaviors until he or she feels safe to share, must be respected. If these characteristics of self-disclosure are not demonstrated during the counseling session, the counselor may interpret these behaviors as resistant and nonproductive. In fact, the counselor may well terminate the counseling services with such justification (LeVine & Padilla, 1980). Such prejudicial action contributes to the substandard counseling services offered to persons of color and others. An aspect of social justice and political equality is the availability of quality counseling services for all persons, regardless of color, age, socioeconomic class, or sexual preference.

Few counselor training programs provide comprehensive preparation concerning multicultural counseling effectiveness. In broad terms, the most devastating consequence of this truth is that the substandard mental health services traditionally offered to persons of color will not improve. Because of the lack of role models in terms of counselors, faculty, and administrators, the traditional white majority student population attending counseling programs will continue. As the status quo continues, persons of power, in terms of curricula content, faculty selection, and the breadth of multicultural instruction, will continue to be members of the white, male, dominant society. The politics of homogeneous interest and control are in power. Although university-level schools of education proclaim the requisite of multicultural training, the power and decision making remains in the hands of administrators and instructors who have limited multicultural sensitivity, knowledge, and skills themselves.

Traditionally, counseling has been willing to accept culturally different peoples if they are willing to become acculturated and reject their cultural distinctiveness. In this way, counselor education is designed to maintain established patterns of dominance, cultural indifference, and behavior control. Some of the negative consequences of counselor educational programs based on a melting pot philosophy are manifested in the use of teaching techniques and materials for counselors, which, though appropriate for middle-class Anglo-Europeans, are inappropriate for other groups. Other consequences are the relative absence of information about the contributions of persons of color to the counseling literature in textbooks and curricula and the possible omission of the self-evaluation of minority clients.

In more focused terms, many problems exist concerning the validity, content, and comprehensiveness of even the "best" multicultural counselor training programs. Many of the programs are "haphazard and fragmented without a strong conceptual framework linked to specific competencies, plus cultural differences are dealt with from an intellectual level without reference to the sociopolitical ramifications of counseling (oppression, discrimination, and racism)" (Sue et al., 1982, p. 477). There is no one training model that seems to encompass all of the necessary components in a way that can be evaluated as effective (McRae & Johnson, 1991). Researchers agree that a comprehensive program trains counselors in three competency areas including sensitivity, knowledge, and skills. The cross-cultural experience cannot be reduced to these three areas; and even if it could be, the counselor must have sufficient breadth and depth in all three areas in order to begin to provide effective counseling to clients of different cultures.

The multicultural counselor training literature has focused on helping *trainees* understand and work with clients who are culturally different. Little emphasis has been placed on helping trainees become aware of themselves as cultural beings. The culturally different client becomes the object to be analyzed and studied, with little focus on the culturally latent values, beliefs, and stereotypes of the counselor.

Thomas Midgette and Sandra Meggert (1991) offer several specific barriers to effective multicultural counseling instruction. They include: (1) the melting pot myth; (2) incongruent student expectations about counseling; (3) overemphasis on verbal self-disclosure; (4) overemphasis on abstract and non-problem-solving strategies; (5) monolingual orientation; (6) overemphasis on long-range goals and the future; (7) lack of understanding of the whole person; (8) lack of understanding of social focus; (9) lack of appreciation for nonverbal communication; (10) an ethnocentric worldview; and (11) ignorance of self-racism and cultural identity of others.

The discussion of the multicultural counseling movement has centered around four key concepts. As a way of review, the concepts are as follows:

1. Multicultural counseling concerns grew out of, first, the changing cultural demographics in the United States, and second, the recognition within the profession that the existing psychological paradigm did not adequately address the mental health needs of people from different cultural backgrounds and other special populations.

2. There is debate among counselor educators as to which multicultural counseling training model best prepares future counselors.

3. The counseling profession is culturally encapsulated and perpetuates racism, and most theories of multicultural counseling seek to adapt existing Euro–North American theories and methods.

4. Ultimately, it has been determined that very few counselor education programs provide comprehensive preparation in multicultural counseling awareness, knowledge, and skills.

The "fourth force" in counseling, multiculturalism, started a critical inquiry into the exclusionary elements of counselor theory and practice. But, it must not stop here. A further look at the psychological theoretical foundations of counselor education proves to unveil even deeper biases that must be addressed.

2

Exclusionary Aspects within Psychological Foundations of Counselor Education

We take a handful of sand from the endless landscape of awareness around us and call that handful of sand the world.

—Robert M. Pirsig
Zen and the Art of Motorcycle Maintenance

The concern and interest surrounding diversity and multiculturalism in counseling has forced a rethinking of the ways in which we counsel clients and educate future counselors. The multicultural movement continues to identify cultural gaps in traditional counselor education curricula. Counselor educators have been forced to look at inherent problems within the theoretical frameworks from which they function. It is time to take a deeper look. This chapter examines issues and problems in the standardization of educational programs and in the psychological foundation of counselor education. Of major concern are the exclusionary aspects of current theory and practice, more specifically, the link between power and knowledge, power and definitions of mental "health," power and practice, and the individual and group oppression brought about by biases in the foundational frameworks of psychology. This closer examination opens the door to a deeper critique of the current philosophy, which in turn advances an agenda of critical thought.

DEFINING COUNSELING IN SCHOOLS

Perhaps a logical approach prior to the discussion of further issues in counselor education is defining what comprises counseling in schools and the role of the school counselor. Counseling in schools differs from counseling conducted in other settings, such as mental health clinics, private practice, and psychiatric hospitals (Baruth & Robinson, 1987; Nugent, 1994). The role of the school counselor has been articulated by the American School Counselor

Association (1990). Although the following narrative is lengthy, it provides a fairly clear picture of school counseling:

The school counselor is a certified professional educator who assists students, teachers, parents, and administrators. Three generally recognized helping processes used by the counselor are counseling, consulting, and coordinating: (1) Counseling is a complex helping process in which the counselor establishes a trusting and confidential working relationship. The focus is on problem-solving, decision-making, and discovering personal meaning related to learning and development; (2) Consultation is a cooperative process in which the counselor-consultant assists others to think through problems and to develop skills that make them more effective in working with students; (3) Coordination is a leadership process in which the counselor helps organize and manage a school's counseling program and related services.

School counselors are employed in elementary, middle/junior high, senior high, and post-secondary schools. Their work is differentiated by attention to age-specific developmental stages of growth and related interests, tasks, and challenges. School counselors are human behavior and relationship specialists who organize their work around fundamental interventions.

Counselor interventions have sometimes been referred to as functions, services, approaches, tasks, activities, or jobs. They have, at times, been viewed as roles themselves, helping to create the image of the counselor. In a comprehensive developmental counseling program, school counselors organize their work schedules around the following basic interventions: individual counseling, small group counseling, large group guidance, consultation, and coordination. (pp. 1–2)

As our society becomes more complex in terms of human relationships, economic fluctuations, increased crime, advanced technology, job market changes, and health care concerns, so too will the role of school counselors become more complex. And, consequently, educating school counselors will become more complex and challenging.

COUNSELOR EDUCATION STANDARDS

In the United States there are approximately 348 colleges and universities that offer a Master's Degree in school counseling, with 25 in the state of California (Hollis & Wantz, 1993). Trends, data, and implications of counselor preparation have been documented through a 23-year longitudinal study. The results of these studies have been articulated in eight national reports. As with all professions, counseling has seen major changes in the last 23 years. Among the most prevalent changes cited are public recognition and acceptance, legislation at the state and national levels, the establishment of state boards for certification, specialization within the profession, the forming of accreditation bodies for the review of preparation programs, increased clinical experience before graduation, increased academic course work, research data to support the effectiveness of counseling, and expanded knowledge bases. One of the trends noted is the prediction that there will be an increase in school counseling programs in the following three years, 1994 to 1997 (Hollis & Wantz, 1993).

The data from the above study strongly indicate a uniformity among the counselor education programs across the country. Similarities were found in admission requirements, the number of academic units, and graduation requirements. The desire for professionalism and consistency among programs has been advanced further by the establishment of guidelines by national accreditation bodies. These guidelines provide standards that are uniformly applied and are high enough that most programs must make changes in order to meet the standards.

This national body is the Council for Accreditation of Counseling and Related Educational Programs (CACREP). CACREP was established in 1981 by the American Counseling Association as a means of strengthening credibility for the profession. As of 1993, 70 of the 348 programs (20%) were CACREP accredited. Between 1990 and 1993, the number of CACREP accredited programs increased by 64 percent, from 45 to 70 programs (Hollis & Wantz, 1993). This trend supports the movement toward continuity among counselor preparation programs.

The CACREP standards are looked upon by counselor educators as defining the optimum in program objectives and curriculum. CACREP standards articulate eight common-core areas of study:

1. HUMAN GROWTH AND DEVELOPMENT—studies that provide an understanding of the nature and needs of individuals at all developmental levels. This area of study includes theories of individual learning, human behavior, and personality development.

2. SOCIAL AND CULTURAL FOUNDATIONS—studies that provide an understanding of issues and trends in a multicultural and diverse society.

3. HELPING RELATIONSHIPS—studies that provide an understanding of counseling and consultation processes.

4. GROUP WORK—studies that provide an understanding of group development, dynamics, counseling theories, group counseling methods and skills, and other group approaches.

5. CAREER AND LIFE-STYLE DEVELOPMENT—studies that provide an understanding of career development and related life factors.

6. APPRAISAL—studies that provide an understanding of individual and group approaches to assessment and evaluation.

7. RESEARCH AND PROGRAM EVALUATION—studies that provide an understanding of types of research methods, basic statistics, and ethical and legal considerations in research.

8. PROFESSIONAL ORIENTATION—studies that provide an understanding of all aspects of professional functioning including history, roles, organizational structures, ethics, standards, and credentialing. (Council for Accreditation of Counseling and Related Educational Programs, 1993, pp. 49–51)

There are several professional benefits which accompany standards in counselor education. First, the standards strengthen the credibility of the profession. Second, they provide guidelines for self-evaluation and improvement for educational programs. Third, standards assure the quality of the institution or the program. Fourth, they provide a systematic way for students to identify programs that maintain high standards. And lastly, they contribute to the unity of the profession.

Yet, there is the potential for a large disadvantage to standardizations among counselor educational programs. There exists a philosophical foundation of counseling that is unquestioningly perpetuated through the adoption of uniform standards. In this case, faculty and students are left with a prescribed, prescripted curricula that may leave little room for critical reflection.

As we approach the twenty-first century, schools face a multitude of problems. Fewer and fewer resources must go farther and farther. At the same time, however, there is a growing concern about the low levels of academic achievement of American children when compared to our world "competitors." Those who do the poorest in academic advancement and who have the highest rates of dropping out of school are children from oppressed minority groups and lower economic status (Pederson & Carey, 1994). Academic achievement and retention of students is of major concern, and effective and responsive counseling in schools is a salient component in the struggle to better serve students who are most likely to drop out. In light of this challenge, the increased complexity of life today, and the counseling demands of the future, it is time to critically question the current philosophical foundations of counselor education.

A CRITIQUE OF TRADITIONAL EDUCATIONAL COUNSELING THEORY

School counselor education in the United States has evolved from general psychological theory as applied to educational settings. There exists a growing homogeneity among programs preparing future counselors that fosters a fairly consistent theoretical foundation. A major component of this book is the examination of the adequacy of the psychological foundation ascribed to by these programs.

As stated, school counselors are human behavior and relationship specialists. Therefore, a large portion of what is taught in counseling programs is psychological and personality theory. Psychological theories are based on how one perceives human nature. The three core schools of psychological theory in counseling are psychoanalytic/psychodynamic, behavioral and cognitive/ behavioral, and humanistic. These core theoretical approaches are briefly described (Nugent, 1994) as follows:

Psychoanalytic/psychodynamic—theories based on the assumption that unconscious drives or instincts influence behavior. The general goal of this approach is to help the client gain insight into his or her unconscious processes. Psychodynamic theories contend that the unconscious is basically positive and the goal is to integrate these impulses into conscious behaviors.

Behavioral/cognitive behavioral—theories based on the assumption that human nature is neutral and adaptive; maladaptive behaviors are learned mainly from a person's responses to or cognition of the environment. Inappropriate behavior is best corrected by reinforcing appropriate behavior and/or improving the person's reasoning or cognitive processes.

Humanistic—theories based on the assumption that people are inherently good and have the power to shape and direct their behavior as they work toward self-actualization. Individuals are seen as active and purposeful with the freedom to make choices about their lives. By getting in touch with one's inherent positive potentialities, self-understanding and self-awareness increase.

Psychology and Power

The wonderment of why, when, and where individuals behave in the ways in which they do has been of fascination for a long time. It is believed that the satisfaction of this wonderment is found in some sort of science. The label of *science* denotes research, truth, predictability, and reliability. A deeper look into the fundamental tenets of psychological theory and practice reveals a dominance of power and control.

The individual subject is the main force driving the study of human nature for the purpose of predicting future behaviors. The discipline of psychology plays an extremely important role in the organization and maintenance of institutions in our society. More specifically, educational psychology has had tremendous influence over the theory and practice in American schools. Henry A. Giroux and Paulo Freire (in Sullivan, 1990) claim:

Operating under the tenets of the natural sciences, the dominant discourses of educational psychology have defined themselves primarily through the appeal to science, objectivity, prediction, and control. While there are strong differences among these discourses, they all share assumptions, methods, and findings that reinforce a reductionistic emphasis on neutrality, objectivity, and instrumentality. More importantly, American educational psychology plays a major role as a discourse of social and cultural reproduction. (p. vii)

In other words, psychology functions in the schools to adapt students to existing relations of power through the use of its power to discipline, test, sort, and label. Historically, there exist specific theoretical assumptions in the study and interpretation of human nature, which, when applied universally to all persons, act as an oppressive force.

Psychology plays a vital role in the maintenance of social order. That is to say, traditional psychological theory and practices as described above have established the norm. These theories work to foster the ongoing life of institutions in their current forms and the ideologies of power that inform them. One of the social ideologies most vehemently rationalized by psychology as we know it is capitalism. This is accomplished through psychology's notion of the individual. As Edmund Sullivan (1990) explains:

Psychology with its notion of the isolated, developing individual allows for the interpretation that all societal problems can be ultimately located at the door of the individual actor. This allows for an interpretation of society as an aggregate of individuals rather than a totality that is much greater than its parts. This fragmented view allows for a way of thinking about society that sidesteps social relationships that go beyond the unit of the individual. To focus on the individual allows one to ignore the complex social dynamics of power that cannot be encapsulated within an individual. (p. xii)

The individual is seen as all responsible for every aspect of his/her nature, emotions, behaviors, and consciousness. The individual is "studied" in order to figure out what makes him/her "tick." The omission of issues dealing with social power, domination, and oppression, along with the focus on the individual, nicely complements the capitalistic ideology of individual financial accomplishment.

Class conflict, racism, patriarchy, and gender are issues which do not appear as areas of study in foundational psychological theory. Psychology, as defined by *Webster's Dictionary* (1989), is the "science of the mind or of the mental states and processes; the science of human nature" (p. 1161). In the name of science, empirical researchers have searched for the "implicit image of man" (De Boer, 1983). There exists a particular human image that best serves a capitalist-patriarchial society, such as that of the United States and Western culture. This image can be described as white, young, male, competitive, individualistic, middle to upper class, heterosexual, and well educated. These characteristics are a mirrored image of the social scientists. Again, the goal was to study the human nature of white, young, competitive, individualistic, middle-class, heterosexual, well-educated men; this was the norm.

A Western version of mental health was derived from these norms (Fernando, 1991). Of major importance to the definition of mental health was, and continues to be, displaying a congruent identity. That is to say, one should not have "multiple personalities" or have highly varied behaviors in different contexts. This would indicate a fragmented person and also an unpredictable person who could be "dangerous." If one did not fit the normative characteristics, for example, being of a non-white race, working class, older, a woman, or valuing group interests over their own (just to name a few), they could have been diagnosed as deficient. If any aspect of a person or his/her culture is perceived as primitive, abnormal, or pathological, the chance is that the person will be tainted by this perception in some way (Fernando, 1991).

Historically, psychology's task has been to manipulate and control behavior. According to Sullivan (1990), psychology "is first and foremost a science of prediction and control of human behavior, rather than one of understanding" (p. xii). This is most evident with behaviorist theory, a common approach in school counseling. The behaviorists not only remove their study of the individual from larger political and social influences, but they also ignore individual intentionality and will. Behavioral psychology sees human beings as concrete things or objects to be manipulated, categorized, and controlled. Just as with Pavlov's dogs, people are viewed as trainable to respond to certain stimuli.

In Western society, the general population is led by the establishment; and in a capitalist society, the establishment is capital. One of the sacrifices made in a capitalist society is that of individual freedom for the freedom of capital (Tolman & Maiers, 1991). It is the power of capital, along with people who control the capital, that makes up the establishment. The bourgeois nature of theory and method centers around their interest to control production and profit. Loren Baritz (1960) draws this conclusion as a result of his study: "Over the years, through hundreds and hundreds of experiments, social scientists have come close to a true science of behavior. They are now beginning to learn how to control conduct. Put this power—genuine, stark, irrevocable power—into the hands of America's managers, and the work that social scientists have done, and will do, assumes implications vaster and more fearful than anything previously hinted" (p. 210).

Just as business owners hold a view of workers as nonfeeling, nonthinking machines that are selected and trained exclusively for the benefit of the employer, so too has the focus of psychology been that of prediction and control. An example is the way independent and dependent variables are used as a way of understanding psychological subject matter. Here it is assumed that the respondents have no history or other reality which may skew the responses. Another example of the control aspect of conventional psychology is the use of the term *subject* when referring to the persons participating in the experiment. Naming people as subjects reduces the human agent to an object that can be manipulated and controlled.

Historically, scientists have categorized the study of psychology as the same as the study of physical and biological sciences. Social scientists have imitated the methodology used in the natural sciences. Consequently, they contend that the study of human behavior is value-free, just as in other sciences. It is as though human agents can and should be studied in much the same way as bacterium and chemicals, in a test tube or a petri dish. A biologist or chemist proceeds with a fastidiously controlled environment and measures, in some sense, the results. The values held by the biologist or chemist have no bearing upon the results. It is easy to conclude, then, that this type of scientific research is value-free. It would be nice to be able to claim that this type of research truly is nonpartisan, but since political interests most often control the scientific research agenda through financial support, one is leery to make such a claim. According to Sullivan (1984), "knowledge is based on a particular *interest* reflected in modern scientific society, and this knowledge-constitutive interest (i.e., technical-control rationality) shapes what counts as knowledge" (p. 5). Therefore, research findings may well mask the political interventions of those in power.

Limiting Metaphors of Psychology

As was indicated, there is a widely accepted and practiced set of psychological theories. Since these theories are presumed to be applicable to nearly all people, it may well be called "mainstream psychology." Even though this psychology is used to understand the common person, uncommon language is used. Most of the language of psychological theory is a formalization of symbols, usually in the form of metaphors. In order to better understand something that is foreign to us, we attempt to identify it with something that is familiar (Sullivan, 1990). This process is metaphorical, meaning that we use metaphors to explain or make clear something of which we know little about. A metaphor, then, is an interaction between symbols. An example of a popular metaphor used in education and in this book is *paradigm* (Kuhn, 1962). This term denotes a fully developed and conscious theoretical perspective, yet often it is loosely used when talking about an educational approach. Sullivan (1990) offers the following explanation:

Our use of this term [metaphor] alerts the reader that we are using language as a "lens" for understanding. To conceive of psychological perspectives as metaphors for understanding means that the problems presented by language affect all theoretical perspectives of whatever variety. Therefore, all theoretical perspectives structure perception and practice as a prism filters light. As a metaphor, theoretical language both reveals and conceals different aspects of human reality. (p. 2)

There are two root metaphors used in conventional psychological theory and practice: the mechanical and the organic (De Boer, 1983; Sullivan, 1990). A third metaphor, the personal, will be introduced later as a metaphor that needs to be added in order to advance psychological theory to relevance in practice.

The first metaphor, the mechanical, attracted human attention during the industrial revolution. The physical sciences developed the notion that the world consists of particles of matter in interaction. As these individual particles are added together, they become a larger totality. These interactions, which make up all of the totalities in the world, are mechanical in nature. In other words, they consist of external influences of one particle upon another. From this perspective, we can view the whole world, including human beings, as nothing more than a complex piece of machinery, a mechanism (Cornforth, 1971). The field of psychology borrowed the mechanical metaphor and began to look at human events and behaviors in much the same way as complex machines. Some behavioralists even refer to humans as "complex robots" (Hull, 1943). Seeing human nature as mechanical material gave way to behavioralist and experimental psychological research. According to Sullivan (1990),

Within the context of the American ethos at the beginning of this century, the budding and neophyte psychological establishment attempted to establish an experimental psychology (i.e., empirical) which would supply the fundamental laws governing all human activity, irrespective of context. Psychology, either knowingly or unknowingly, was entrenched in the American socioeconomic order, and its more articulate spokesperson would express themselves as creating a science that would control the labor and capital. (p. 4)

The typical empirical–analytical psychological image of man and woman is that he/she exists in the same manner as a thing (De Boer, 1983). Test persons are viewed as "things-with-properties." Behavior is seen as a reaction to stimuli in order to reestablish a balance. People, then, function in much the same way as a robot, an image of men and women that neglects a person's autonomous activity. Theo De Boer (1983) expands this notion: "Nurture then is nothing more than training in the appropriate reaction to the environment, beginning with the toilet training of children—and ending in adult man in an affluent society, which makes everybody happy, conditioning him, in a strictly scientific manner, through the mass media to be the perfect consumer—that is, an automation properly answering in the ways prescribed by the industrial-military-political establishment" (p. 6). As an attempt to discover the universal laws (absolute truth) of human behavior, experiments with test persons are conducted by those who claim to be unbiased, neutral scientists. The test person in the experiment is subjected to an artificial situation in order to determine the law-governed relations between the variables in conduct. According to De Boer (1983), "The test person is exposed to circumstances that he has not created himself or does not fully understand, to which he then reacts in a deterministic manner" (p. 6). Consequently, as long as the test person is considered a mechanical being, he/she is stripped of all history and social influences. In other words, they are seen as ahistorical and asocial.

In traditional psychology, the principle of analysis, the experiment, is underscored as *the way* to knowing truth. In order to explain events, scientists manipulate, predict, and control supposedly decomposing conditions. Therefore, *"Explanation* of a phenomenon involves an attempt to manipulate, control, and predict antecedent—consequent conditions with a view to defining linear causality. Causality is a relationship between antecedent conditions and consequences. Manipulation and control assume the ability to control some conditions in nature, to vary these conditions while holding other conditions constant, and then to observe differential consequences in this controlled setting" (Sullivan, 1990, p. 3).

The driving force of such experiments is the ability to predict; high prediction comes from a good explanation of an event and therefore gives credence to a particular psychological theory. "The experiment is a reflection of a culture whose reference point is a rationality based on technical control" (Sullivan, 1990, p. 5). This concept underscores a critical positioning that knowledge is power; knowledge is political. Michel Foucault (1980) comments, "Knowledge and power are integrated with one another, and there is no point in dreaming of a time when knowledge will cease to depend on power; this is just a way of reviving humanism in a utopian guise. It is not possible for power to be exercised without knowledge, it is impossible for knowledge not to engender power" (p. 52).

In the context of psychological research, those in charge of the experiments hold forms of power that work to support particular interests in modern society. It is important to note that, since researchers fail to question or unmask such power, they are unaware of their participation in power structures or the societal ramifications of their work. In a strange way, experiments mirror oppressive aspects of society. As expounded upon by De Boer (1983):

Through its apparently purely intellectual approach, science legitimizes a harsh reality of life in society—the fact that man [woman] is treated as an object. Habermas was the first to point this out. This ideology must be conceived of along the following lines. It seems entirely reasonable to treat man [woman] like an object in an experiment. If one lives in a society in which the "objectification" of man [woman] is commonplace, there is a strong temptation to interpret the experiment situation as a legitimatization of such a society. (p. 7)

The second metaphor utilized in orthodox psychology is organic and refers to the process or products of life—in human beings, animals, or plants (Williams, 1976). Here, human beings are seen as *organisms,* since an organism has no history but only reacts according to clearly established patterns (Holzkamp, 1976). Such beliefs bring about the "organism ideology" of psychology. The identifiable difference between the mechanical and the organic metaphor is that an organism is a living thing with the ability to transform itself in order to survive its changing environment. A prime example of a theoretical application of the organic metaphor is Darwin's theory of evolution.

Sullivan (1990) identifies two contemporary movements that embody elements of the organic metaphor: structuralism and functionalism. In the late

1950s and early 1960s, new theoretical shifts were taking place in American psychology as well as fields of study. The new challenge to mechanistic theories was structuralism (some also refer to this movement as modernism). This approach assumes that a structure (in whatever form it takes) is a totality. Another way to put it is that the whole *is more than the sum of its parts.* A structure, which often contains "stages," as seen in the works of Piaget, Kohlberg, and Erikson, is a holistic organism. There are four salient characteristics of a structure, as defined by structuralists:

Structure as a synthetic principle is diametrically opposite to analyses, as exemplified by even the most complex behavior theories. A structure is a holistic entity characterized by *internal* dependencies. This is explicated by Piaget, for example, in his definition of a structure as a system of transformations which, as a system, implies a lawfulness of organization independent of the elements that compose it. This system is characterized as a totality. In other words, whatever the composing elements in the system, they are subordinated to the laws defining the system as a system. In addition, a system is characterized by multiple transformations that are interdependent on the structure itself. Finally, a structure is self-regulating and tends toward the conservations and enhancement of the system itself. (Sullivan, 1990, p. 10)

Structuralism brought a new vocabulary to the psychological exchange. This shift included terms such as "wholes," "interdependent structures," "open systems," "feedback," "information," and "communication" (Wilden, 1975). Structuralism brought great change to psychology, particularly educational psychology, with a shift from classical logical empiricism to adopting an interpretive language from biology.

The second movement in psychology which incorporates an organic metaphor is functionalism. This position considers the mental processes of sense perception, emotion, volition, and thought as functions of the biological organism. In the psychological arenas, this orientation involves the identification and interpretation of human "traits." These traits are believed to be adaptive or maladaptive for individual and societal survival; they are considered to be adaptive organs (Sullivan, 1990).

Clearly the most prominent human trait to be studied by psychologists is intelligence. There has been, and continues to be, great controversy over test bias, the pretense of neutrality, the interpretation of test results, and the political misuse of supposed test results. According to Sullivan (1990), "The assumptions of what was adaptive or maladaptive were defined in an ethnocentric manner unknown to the testers, since they assumed a certain world view as superior (i.e., white, Anglo-Saxon)" (p. 13).

Psychologists also have been interested in the trait differences between men and women. Again we find functionalism as scientists delve into the biological characteristics of gender. An example of such research is the study of women's motives to "avoid success" (Horner, 1972). Here the belief is that women have a social/psychological trait which reduces achievement in social settings and accounts for their lack of success.

A newer approach to structuralism is a redirected focus from cognitive traits to personality traits. The inquiry called sociobiology looks at traits that encourage the coming together of human groups, such as altruism, and those traits that discourage group cohesiveness, such as aggression and competition. A major reason for this type of study was a perception that social cultural solidarity was threatened due to the encouragement of severe individualism (Campbell, 1975). There is an assumption that humans tend to be self-involved because biological evolution would choose these traits as a result of genetic tension between selfish and altruistic traits, thus maintaining social order.

When the only metaphors used to interpret the psychology of humans are mechanical and organic, the concept of men and women is reduced. Among the important missing aspects are the influence and power of culture, experience, changing human perceptions, and the ability for men and women to alter their lived experiences. There are certain aspects of human behavior that can be understood by the use of these metaphors, yet they are restrictive in nature.

Biases in Psychology

In addition to the limiting nature of the metaphors used in mainstream psychological theory and practice, one also can find major biases. Some examples are the failure to link psychology to a social order; the omission of issues regarding ethnicity, gender, and social class; the universal use of tests and assessments that are normed by white middle-class men; and the cultural and gender biases in definitions of mental health, emotional health, and illness.

Failing to link a person's psychological profiles with social structures leads to "blaming the victim." Within the framework of an individualistic theory, it is the responsibility of the individual to work harder, smarter, and so on, in order to succeed. It is assumed that the person has total command over his/her human situation with intentional control. There exist social structural conditions that unconsciously operate as potent determinants of human action, yet these are not examined in conventional psychology. A case in point is a study (Brenner, 1976) which found that changes in the economy, specifically in the level of unemployment, are the single most important source of changing rates of admission to mental hospitals. There is also a positive correlation between hospital admittance and class structure. Psychiatric problems increase as economic resources decline, and mental illness drops when employment conditions improve, even when there has been no therapeutic intervention. Any psychological theme that tends to blame the victim for lack of intentional control is oppressive.

Psychologists, as individuals, and institutions are linked to specific social orders, and the kind of work they do will be imprinted by that social order

(Sarason, 1981). This leads to the researchers having the existing power arrangements reflected in their theorizing. Psychology as a form of social inquiry will reflect social currents in its theory and practice. For example, during the early 1970s, when women, gays, and lesbians pushed for liberation, the psychological community began to reconsider their focus on research and practice to that of a more liberal stance.

As is suggested here, there exist biases in psychology which relate to social order. In other words, the bias in psychology reflects the biases of the larger culture. According to Sullivan (1990), "psychological interpretation will normally be a complementary horizon to the status quo, psychological expertise functioning as a form of legitimation or rationalization for the normative order or status quo" (p. 139). Following this line of thinking, one can conclude that the psychological interpreter must reflect a bias of viewpoint in his/her interpretation, even though contemporary psychology claims value neutrality.

Due to the main focus of contemporary psychology being that of the individual, issues relating to power structures are either ignored or attributed in some way back to the individual. For example, instead of examining the power status of men over women in society, one hypothesis is that women have an avoidance of success trait (Horner, 1972). In addition to gender, social class and race are structures of domination from which investigators in psychology abstain, for the preservation of the individual.

Psychology as a form of disciplined inquiry fails to recognize its social class origin and in practice ignores its affects (Sullivan, 1990). By education, training, and income, psychologists and school counselors are embedded in the dynamics of the middle class. Even though psychologists claim to maintain professional distance, they cannot detach themselves from the influence of their unexamined social class status. In fact, psychologists and counselors usually attribute social class dynamics to intrapsychic factors (Ryan, 1974) since the unit of analysis in which they are trained is the individual. Such training tends to mask or hide the effects of social class structure on personal development.

Prior to the women's movement of the early 1970s, the psychological uniqueness and needs of women for the most part were either ignored, seen as a derivative or accidental by-product of a larger theory (Sullivan, 1990), or a concept called *abstract universality* was applied (Gould, 1976). Here abstract universality means lacking specificity, viewing gender as accidental and unnecessary components of truth. Examples of abstract universality in contemporary psychological theory are superabundant. Most prevalent personality theorists, cutting across theoretical orientations, apply some version of universal abstraction. Among these theorists are Carl Jung, Alfred Adler, Erik Erikson, Abraham Maslow, B. F. Skinner, and Carl Rodgers, all of whom are studied as part of counselor education.

Carl Jung's "collective unconscious" concept, which contends that all persons have an inaccessible level of the psyche—the collective or transpersonal unconscious—is an excellent example of abstract universality. Jung believed that we all have universal experiences which leave their imprints on each person at birth. His fundamental belief was that "since all people face essentially the same experiences, these universal experiences determine how we will perceive and react to our own world" (Schultz, 1986, p. 83).

A second example of abstract universality is Erik Erikson's psychosocial developmental stage theory. Here it is believed that personal progress is accomplished through a series of stages that are identical for all persons. Additionally, individuals advance through these stages at approximately the same age. Erikson's theory has had a profound influence on counseling theory and practice, perhaps more so than any other (Blocher, 1974; Rodgers, 1984). It is important to note that, although he acknowledged style differences in men and women, he left the theory completely intact. In effect, Erikson excluded the female perspective and lived experiences of psychosocial development. This omission allowed for a "cleaner" theory that offered universal application. The final result is a theory that has been extensively applied to all, regardless of gender, culture, race, economic class, or sexual orientation. More recent research suggests a revision of Erikson's theory which contains a focus on the anchoring role of relationships in women's lives (Josselson, 1987). And further, there is an association between a relational identity with women's ability to learn through connections with others (Belenkey, Clinchy, Goldberger, & Tarule, 1986). Yet, because these insights are not part of the mainstream psychological belief system, nor are they fully embraced by conventional counselor educators, they are seldom explored by counseling students.

The application of unquestioned abstract universality diffuses aspects of gender, ethnicity, culture, and other salient issues that may greatly influence human nature. The interpretive horizon of this concept reflects the interests, needs, and prejudices of particular social groups (Gould, 1976). These prejudices produce distortions in our understanding of what is important, which leads to a form of essentialism. Here, essentialism refers to a doctrine that certain traditional concepts, ideals, and skills are essential to society and should be taught methodically to all students, regardless of individual needs, ability, and so on. Furthermore, "essentialism reflects such interests in a particularly harmful way, because it tends to mask them under the guise of universality and therefore is deceptive" (Gould, 1976, p. 17). Contemporary psychological concepts and practices are skewed with the interpretational formulation of "one gender, one race, one sexual orientation, one class," and so on. This monoperspective excludes differences and hence is oppressive in nature.

The concept of abstract universality was confronted as the women's movement and feminist psychology began to take shape, draw attention, and gain power. Feminists contend that the psychological outlooks have been the artifact of Western culture under the dominance of white males who have assumed themselves to be speaking in a universal human voice. As is succinctly expressed by Miriam Greenspan (1983),

Psychological differences between the sexes both reflect and perpetuate the structurally unequal distribution of power in the society. Men and women psychically structured along gender lines tend to see themselves in ways that do not threaten the social order but perpetuate it. Traditional psychology theories of women have also reflected the interests of men. They have been theories made by men about women, made by the dominating group about the dominated. In this sense, psychology as we know it also tends to reflect and perpetuate the subordination of women. (p. 34)

The feminist view and critique of psychology questions the social implications of theory and practice. This critique unmasks ways in which women have been consistently excluded from the centrally important metaphysical, epistemological, moral, and political conceptions of personhood. Feminists make a strong case that men have held power to name or define what it means to be human, adult, intelligent, moral, successful, and other appropriatenesses. These names and definitions are the response of *men's* experiences of and need for separateness and distinctiveness (Greenspan, 1983). In early psychological research, men held the power and authority in society, and they defined what it meant to be a "normal" man and woman. By asking biased questions, using unrepresented samples (all male), interpreting data subjectively, and explaining results inappropriately, researchers developed and established exclusionary theoretical foundations. An example of such skewed research is Lawrence Kohlberg's (1981) study of moral development. Even though his study was limited to 50 male children and adolescents, his theory has been applied universally to males and females and his work has been basic to some widely used values clarification assessments (Nugent, 1994).

As women began to identify biases in psychotherapy, they also made attempts to reshape personality theory. Early reviews of personality theory (Doherty, 1973) were highly critical of Freudian concepts such as penis envy, castration anxiety, and the Electra Complex. Later, limitations identified in more contemporary theories, such as Kolberg, Levison, and Perry, were based on formative empirical research of white middle-class men (Miller, 1976; Gilligan, 1977) that were then generalized to women. Yet, even with the feminist movement and advances made in the field, one might note that all but one theorist identified as providing impetus for this book is male.

Like gender, most of the classical texts on personality do not include the construct of ethnicity and/or race. According to Sullivan (1990), "the work of treating ethnicity or race has traditionally fallen to sociologists and anthropologists who treat race within the context of culture" (p. 117). This is not to say that ethnicity has not been of influence in the development of psychology. The psychological testing movement in North America was in part advanced by the screening of immigrants through the use of standardized tests of intelligence (Sullivan, 1990). Standardized tests were seen as a way of creating universalistic norms for the assessment of intellectual abilities. The erroneous assumption that standardized tests, as well as traditional psychology theory and practice, are "culture-free" is an additional example of universal abstracts, as was discussed previously.

Determining the extent of bias and exclusionary aspects in counseling theory and practice needs to be a critical agenda item for counselor educators. Theories taught today are based on the experience of only one segment of society; a solo voice of reality is heard (Lee & Richardson, 1991; Sue, 1981). One major assumption is about "what constitutes mental health and mental illness, how illness should be treated, and how counselors should be trained" (Ritchie, 1994). How mental and emotional health are defined greatly determines counseling theory and practice since it may well define the goal of therapy. When the definitions are restrictive and biased in favor of a particular group, unfair assumptions about the health of members of other groups occur.

Assumptions about normal behavior are tied to cultural and gender biases. It is assumed that those who are mentally and emotionally healthy are portrayed as being independent, self-confident, assertive, and having an internal locus of control (Pederson, 1987; Usher, 1989). If one is "healthy," they are in control of their lives, self-sufficient, competitive, and able to change themselves or influence others in order to better get along in their worlds (Althen, 1981). What is seen as less healthy are behaviors such as connectedness, cooperativeness, stability, and external locus of control. It is important to note that these "less psychologically healthy" characteristics are valued by other cultures and are identified with female gender roles (Althen, 1981; Cook, 1992; Sue, 1981). Martin Ritchie (1994) sums up this issue well:

The dangers in uncritically accepting definitions of mental and emotional health that may be biased are many. These definitions are used as outcome measures in evaluating the effectiveness of counseling treatments. They are used for the construction of psychological tests and inventories, which in turn are used to screen and diagnose people [Pederson, 1987]. They form the basic assumptions of many of our counseling theories [Lee & Richardson, 1991]. Some counseling strategies and techniques are predicated on helping people assume the traits inherent in these definitions. (p. 345)

Yet, the unmasking of such biases will be accomplished only by changing the questions asked about psychological theories and practice. Instead of asking, "how can I get my client to change to fit the theory or definition?" we need to teach counseling students to ask questions such as, "in what ways does this theory favor one group or world view which marginalizes my client?" The unquestioning of current definitions of psychological health leads to the mislabeling of certain persons and groups as less healthy than others. Again, according to Ritchie (1994), "Once a trait is uncritically accepted as indicative of psychological health, measures of that trait are used to correlate and validate other measures of psychological health. This could conceivably create the false impression that certain traits are valid measures of mental and emotional health because of the number of tests or outcome studies using those traits" (p. 346).

A clear example of such potential bias can be found in the standard for defining mental and emotional disorders in the counseling field, the *Diagnostic and Statistical Manual of Mental Disorders* (4th ed., rev., [DSM-IV]; American Psychiatric Association, 1994). This last revision, completed in 1994, was attributable to numerous complaints that previous versions were full of biases against ethnic and cultural groups as well as women. A case in point is the DSM-III-R diagnostic category, "self-defeating personality disorder." Feminist critics contended that 85 percent of normally socialized women display many of the passive behavioral criteria of this disorder. Self-defeating personality disorder is presumed to be a disease or character disorder rooted in dysfunctional family patterns (Van Wormer, 1989). According to Carolyn Enns (1993), "It obscures complex, real-life situations and gender role injunctions, ignores power differentials in relationships, and leads to an overemphasis on individual solutions rather than to social change and justice" (p. 19). Caution must always be taken when using diagnostic categories to label people, as they could support additional discrimination against and revictimization of individuals and groups. Further, "as a consequence of using these procedures, it is inevitable that clients who do not share a Eurocentric world view are at risk for having their presenting problems [i.e., mental health problems] inadequately identified or entirely obscured. They are at risk for pathologization, caricature, or dehumanization" (Dana, 1993, p. 92).

Even with the controversy, the DSM remains the standard diagnostic measure that is used universally to label people with their disorders. This results in a disproportionate number of people being condemned to diagnoses of mental illness when, perhaps, their behavior is "healthy" when placed within the context of their culture, circumstance, or life-style (Velsquez, Johnson, & Brown-Cheatham, 1993).

Traditional psychological theory has been created from the analysis of isolated moments of human action as opposed to a reflection of human behavior that is embedded in a personal history and is socially influenced. Several scholars have challenged the conventional views with the hope of transforming the field of psychology. Unfortunately, this advancement in psychological theory has barely surfaced in educational counseling.

The key concerns raised in this chapter center around the exclusionary aspects of the psychological foundations of counselor education. For clarification and enumeration, the following are the core concepts identified and discussed:

1. The potential for continued teaching of theoretical limitations to future counselors due to counselor education program standardization in the United States.

2. The oppressive results of embedded power structures within traditional psychological theory, research, and practice.

3. The oppressive results of excluding the lived realities of women, people of color, gays and lesbians, the working class, and others from the foundations of psychology.

4. The oppressive and exclusionary results of using limited metaphors and notions of abstract universality to understand human nature.

5. The oppressive and exclusionary results when there is a strong adherence to rigidly defined norms within the constructs of "healthy" emotions, personality, identity, behaviors, values, beliefs, life-styles, and gender roles.

In light of this critique of traditional counselor education psychological theory, coupled with the issues raised surrounding multicultural counseling, it can be strongly concluded that failing to critically question the theoretical foundation that informs counseling practice has resulted in disenfranchising, oppressing, and silencing those students who are of the highest risk of failing in school. Therefore, *inclusionary*, as opposed to *exclusionary,* ideologies must be incorporated into counselor education. In the struggle for equality, counselors must be comfortable with the discomfort that comes as a result of deconstructing previously held truths. Yet, in order for these transformations to occur, counselor educators must embrace the political project of a pedagogy that frames a discourse of possibilities—a pedagogy that reveals the exclusions, questions the power of norms, and charts a journey toward liberatory action. Such a pedagogy can be created through the exploration of critical theory.

3

Forming a Language of Analysis: Critical Theory

> Every thought, idea, and particular is interwoven with the whole societal process. Critical theory, in spite of its efforts to reflect the object in its manifold forms of development, depends in its every step on particular historical conditions. Its content is ever changing.
>
> —David Held
> *Introduction to Critical Theory*

Embedded within counselor education is the de-emphasis of the relationship between power and knowledge. Although in the new multicultural counseling literature (Pederson, 1994) and in at least one introductory counseling textbook (Nugent, 1994) there is mention of the existence of a powerful dominant societal culture, there fails to be a wide acknowledgment of the issue. This is because the fundamental theoretical bases from which counselors are trained and practice do not question such links and therefore do not confront the oppressive results. Within the questioning of the dynamics between power and knowledge, a new language in which to frame questions for critical analysis of counselor education emerges. A solid grounding in critical ideologies has the potential to bring about a shift in the way one views and interprets their world. Although some critical images and notions are complex, and the words used may at first seem foreign, the collective results of understanding this material are worth the exploration.

The purpose of this chapter is to articulate more specific and detailed characteristics of a critical theoretical platform for the purpose of revealing not only more exclusionary aspects of counseling, but also to map out changes that are needed in counselor education. Critical theory is an "attempt to understand the oppressive aspects of society in order to generate societal and individual transformation" (Tierney, 1993, p. 4).

CRITICAL THEORY

The philosophical foundation of critical ideology is derived from a somewhat unorthodox interpretation of Marxist theory. The founders of critical theory placed history at the center of their approach to philosophy and society. The following is a brief overview of Marxist theory and the consequential historical development of critical theory.

In 1848, the existing order throughout Europe was challenged, and sometimes overturned, only to be back again a few months later. The turbulent social issues were nationalism, constitutional government, broadened suffrage, and the abolition of serfdom in the Balkans. The enemies of the time were the ruling class, the Catholic Church, and the Hapsburg influence. As a result, serfs were freed, but the dreams of liberalism and good government faded away. The French Revolution left a residue of class hatred and a new toughness of mind that set the stage for Marxism.

Marxism

The historical foundations of all critical thought, whether it be pedagogy, theory, or psychology, come out of the early philosophical notions of Karl Marx. Unfortunately, most know and understand little about Marxism, except that it denotes communism, which to the Western culture is abhorrent. So here the reader may need to pause and make a shift of his/her own, in order to be open to the application of Marxism to critical discourse. Marx believed that the nature of the world is material. That is, systems establish and perpetuate a hierarchical structure among members of society in order to be sustained.

Karl Marx, a German philosopher, argued that economic relationships are the basic forces of history, and that it is only around them that the whole complex of social relationships arise. For the Marxist, the way people think, perceive, and feel—that is, their "consciousness"—is related to the basic mode of economic production in their society. In other words, fundamental ideas about the nature of truth and falsity, about goodness and beauty, can be best understood by examining the way in which production is carried on at a particular time. The only way to understand the basic concepts by which we organize our conceptual, ethical, and aesthetic worlds is to examine our relationship to the productive possibilities of the society. In Marxist theory, truth is dependent on the concepts that culture makes available to one (Feinberg & Soltis, 1992).

As a society develops and changes, the concepts in that culture also change, which allows individuals to think in new ways. For the Marxist, the way to understand changes in the characteristics of thought is to explore the changes in the mode of production. A hypothetical example would be a society in which all of their needs for food, shelter, and other items can no longer be provided for within the boundaries of their self-contained area. In order for this group to survive, they must search out new resources. What once was their concrete understanding of space and direction, such as boundaries of their "land," now must change in order to allow them to travel for the purpose of meeting material needs. Therefore, because they must find a new mode (travel direction and distance) of production, a change in their thinking must take place. Thus, conceptual differences evolve historically within a group.

Marx had an explanation for the different ways of thinking that is found among different groups existing within the same society during the same historical period. Marxists explain this by using the concept of social class. A class society is created whenever people are related in different ways to the means of production, and each particular class is defined in terms of this relationship. For example, in a capitalist society, where the means of production are owned by individuals who hire workers to produce the commodity, the "workers" will constitute a different class than the owners. Since identification with a particular class is defined only in terms of the relation its members have with production, a class may consist of many different kinds of people. For example, the working class will have people of different races, religions, and nationalities. The shared working class interests are not always recognized due to these differences. Membership within a particular class entails more than the relationship with production. Members of a class share certain values, a certain outlook, and a set of perceptions and ideas about the nature of social life. In other words, each class holds a certain "class consciousness" (Feinberg & Soltis, 1992).

False Consciousness and Hegemony

In some cases, a society will work to block the development of class consciousness because the class may exert its collective power for its own interest. When this occurs, progressive social change may be hindered.

Marxists use the notions of *false consciousness* and *hegemony* to describe how this happens. According to Walter Feinberg and Jonas Soltis (1992),

Members of the subordinate class who express their point and share values of the dominant class exhibit false consciousness. True consciousness of your own class is impeded by your acceptance of the values of the dominant class. When the dominant class is successful in establishing its own mode of thinking among most members of the subordinate class, it is said to have established hegemony over the subordinate class. Hegemony means having a preponderance of influence and authority over others. This influence is expressed both in the concepts and the institutional arrangements of the social structure. (p. 50)

An example of false consciousness is the slave who adopts the values of the master. The slave believes that he or she is the property of the master, to do with as the master wishes. There is a hegemonic process when one class controls the thinking of another class through such cultural forms as the church, the media, or the schools.

According to Peter McLaren (1989), hegemony "is a struggle in which the powerful win the consent of those who are oppressed, with the oppressed unknowingly participating in their own oppression" (p. 173). He goes on to say that "hegemony refers to the moral and intellectual leadership of a dominant class over a subordinate class achieved not through coercion (i.e., threat of imprisonment or torture) or the willful construction of rules and regulations (as in dictatorship or fascist regime), but rather through the general winning of consent of the subordinate class to the authority of the dominant class" (p. 174). The subordinate class actively subscribes to many of the values and objectives of the dominant class, not knowing that the source of the values and interests that informs them is the dominant class. Therefore, there is no imposed force needed from the dominant class in order to evoke hegemonic powers.

Production and Social Change

Orthodox Marxists believe that all social change is rooted in the way in which people produce their goods. In turn, new productive methods open up the possibility for positive human development. The way that the political, legal, religious, and educational systems serve to enhance or to hinder human development in any given historical period must be understood. This means that a particular system which serves a progressive role in society may come to serve a negative influence when there are changes in the modes of production.

In order to clarify this concept, think for a moment about the invention, production, and distribution of television. Across America, excitement and desire for television soared, as well as support of in-the-home visual electric entertainment. One result of this new product was increased contact and interaction with persons around the world. Suddenly, different cultures, beliefs, and ways of life were introduced and viewed in the comfort of living rooms. Viewers slowly began to change the ways they perceived different parts and peoples of the world. What was once unknown became the topic of family conversations. As long as television worked to increase awareness, acceptance, and understanding of human differences, it may be said that it was a promoter of positive human development, thus serving a progressive role in society.

Of course, due to the high cost of this new invention, the only class within the society who could readily afford a television was the "upper class." Owning a television became a status symbol of wealth. Those who promoted and profited most from the capital gains of television wanted to please the viewing public; therefore, programs that symbolized the dreams and desires of society were aired. The most desirous life-style in a capitalist society is that of "white" wealth and status; therefore, television programs mirrored that which was most accepted by the viewers. Television owners could sit in their homes and watch themselves. As the production of televisions became more advanced and the prices dropped.

more people were able to purchase them. By this time, the belief that one must have a television was a powerful motivator. Now members of the working class were able to "watch" the wealthy class live, close up and personal. A Marxist would contend that this resulted in the thinking of the working class being controlled through the media of television by the dominant class, and hence hegemony occurred. According to McLaren (1989), there exists an embedded ability in the dominant culture to "frame" and define what the *proper* family, career, household, and emotions are for everyone. The dominant culture provides the terms of reference, such as images, visions, stories, and ideals, by which we all are judged. Through this power comes the expectations and aspirations that create a common world view. As long as there is a standard, expected world view, relations of power and privilege are disguised. This common world view is communicated and articulated through the mass media, schools, and government institutions (McLaren, 1989).

As was mentioned earlier, hegemony always serves to hinder human development. So even though at one historical moment television may have served a positive role in human development, due to a change in new production methods and an increase in access, a hegemonic influence resulted on subordinate groups.

Ideology

Hegemony would be powerless without ideology. Ideology imbues all aspects of social life. As explained by McLaren (1989), "Ideology refers to the production and representation of ideas, values, and beliefs and the manner in which they are expressed and lived out by both individuals and groups. Simply put, ideology refers to the production of sense and meaning" (p. 176). Ideology is the result of the intercrossing of power and meaning in the context of society. An ideology can be thought of as a framework of thought. It is through these frameworks of thought that societies explain, figure out, and make sense of (or give meaning to) their social and political worlds. We tend to accept as normal and as common sense these sometimes complex systems of ideas, social practices, symbols, and rituals (McLaren, 1989). If we did not have these frameworks, we could not make sense of our world; although with them, our perceptions are skewed in a direction that is most accepted within the social realm.

Ideology can have both a negative and a positive consequence at any given time. According to McLaren (1989), the positive function of ideology "is to provide the concepts, categories, images, and ideas by means of which people make sense of their social and political world, form projects, come to a certain consciousness of their place in the world and act in it" (pp. 176–177). The negative consequence of ideology is the selectivity of the perspectives. The theory of domination adds greater understanding to the negative function of ideology. Explained by McLaren (1989), "Domination occurs when relations of power established at the institutional level are systematically asymmetrical; that is, when they are unequal, therefore privileging some groups over others" (p. 177).

Further, ideology functions negatively in four different ways: legitimation, dissimulation, fragmentation, and reification.

Legitimation occurs when that which is in some sort of power is maintained by being percieved as having worth (McLaren, 1989). For instance, by legitimizing the court system as just and fair, as giving everyone the opportunity for equal defense and "their day in court," the dominant society hides the truth that those with affluence often obtain the better defense and assistance in a very complex and intimidating system. Another example is the legitimizing of schools as giving the same opportunity to all; yet through hidden aspects of the curricula which teach from the lofty white perspective, those who benefit most are those of affluence.

Dissimulation occurs when associations of domination are concealed, denied, or obscured in various ways. A prime example is the practice of tracking students in schools; either college bound or vocational training bound. Schools claim that this is a way to best serve students of varying academic abilities. Yet, most often, it is the students of working-class families and bicultural backgrounds who are funneled toward vocational training, thus maintaining a flow of workers willing to accept menial occupations. Another way of looking at tracking is that it is a way to mask a mechanism of sorting students by social class, thus covering a socially reproductive function (McLaren, 1989).

Fragmentation is a way in which relations of domination are sustained by the production of meanings in a fashion that fragments groups, thus creating opposing groups. An example cited by McLaren (1989) is when conservative educational critics blame the accommodation of low-income bicultural students for the declining standards in education. A common result is that subordinate groups become antagonistic with immigrant students, thus preventing oppressed groups from working collectively for their rights.

The last mode of negative ideology is *reification*. This occurs when temporary historical situations are presented as permanent, natural, and commonsensical--as if they exist outside of time. For instance, as part of the doctoral curricula at a leading graduate school, students are encouraged to read and synthesize a number of prescribed "great books." These works are respected by the faculty as high status knowledge since through recent history they have been selected for study by leading institutions. The preselection of these specific works, regardless of the possible changes in ideology, have a stamp of approval as permanent bodies of truth. Since they have been declared as "great works" by powerful universities, it seems only logical that they continue to be assigned reading for new scholars. The assignment of these books perpetuates the notion of what is "culturally literate" in the dominant society and negates other ways of knowing. Teaching from these books is a way of injecting certain values, beliefs, and behaviors, thereby solidifying the existing social hierarchy (McLaren, 1989). Hence, these "great books" reify the dominant ideology and could prevent progressive ideology development.

There exists in America a *dominant ideology* consisting of the beliefs and values shared by the majority of the population. For example, the majority of Americans, regardless of degree of affluence, share the belief that democratic socialism is inferior to capitalism, or that being young is better than being a senior citizen, or that men should hold positions of power and intelligence, such as president of the nation, and women should be the prime caregivers to children. The economic system needs consumer capitalism to sustain it; therefore, it seems commonsensical to uphold loyalty in capitalism. Also, because men have always held the highest positions of power, it seems only logical that this is the best for all. And likewise, because of the prevailing hegemony, the ideology of "man being head of the household" and "the bread winner" is necessary to keep the economy stable (McLaren, 1989). These ideas have been nurtured and perpetuated for decades through the mass media, the schools, and through family socialization.

Marxists contend that new social ideas or codes are developed by and for a specific social class. Because the development of new codes always involves a struggle with other classes, the notion of "universal principle" is often invoked. This means that the new idea is sold under the premise that it promises to serve the interest of all, not just the interest of the rising class. An example offered by Feinberg and Soltis (1992) is as follows:

In American history, the principles of "life, liberty, and the pursuit of happiness" were not explicitly articulated as serving the interests of only a specific class of people, even though the founding fathers had common interests as slave owners and large property holders. Rather these ideals were formulated to appeal to as wide a range of individuals as possible. They were expressed as universal rights that would advance the position of everyone against what was seen by some as oppressive taxation and arbitrary rule by the monarchy. (p. 5)

Universal Principles and the Law of Contradiction

Universal principles work to enlist the support of many dissatisfied elements of society. The flip side of it is that a new set of standards is created that eventually may be used to judge the emerging order and its newly advantaged class. Going back to the example in American history, after 100 years, the United States experienced a war over slavery. And yet even today, many bicultural groups, women, gays, and lesbians do not experience freedom and equality.

America's universal principle of life, liberty, and the pursuit of happiness creates a society in which people believe that talent should determine social and economic position. Marxists believe that this principle is best seen "historically as a weapon in a class struggle used first to overcome an assigned place in life and used later by the newly advantaged groups to maintain their gains and by the still disadvantaged ones to assert their claims to equal treatment" (Feinberg & Soltis, 1992, p. 53).

A fundamental law in Marxist theory is the *law of contradiction*. This law affirms that each social group contains within it the seeds of its own destruction and transcendence. There is a natural law working within oppressed peoples that gives them the ability to recognize when they are being exploited, create a united consciousness, and revolt for liberation. On the other hand, each social form also has the seed of destruction. Marxists believe that if this law was not present, then basic social change would not occur and class power would prevail (Feinberg & Soltis, 1992).

Neo-Marxism

Less traditional, newer forms of Marxism are concerned with issues related not only to economic oppression, but also to domination by classes in noneconomic social forms. These Marxists contend that there is a need to critically analyze each situation of domination in its own terms. This means not presupposing that the cause of the domination or inequality always has an economic base. Some contend that contemporary social domination is present in communication modalities as much as in economic structures (Feinberg & Soltis, 1992). Because of this, it is just as important to examine the control of information as it is the control of production. Since the media and the schools are major arteries of communication in this society, they must be critiqued from a Marxist framework.

The Historical Reexamination of Marxism

The changing and challenging historical circumstances in Europe in the 1920s and 1930s invoked theorists to question the political, economic, and social conditions of the time. The stage was set for a rethinking of Marxist theory and practice. George Lukacs and Karl Korsch were among the first to reexamine the application of Marxist theory to contemporary social themes (Held, 1980). According to Lukacs, the purpose of theory is "to analyze and expose the hiatus between the actual and the possible, between the existing order of contradictions and a potential future state. Theory must be oriented, in short, to the development of consciousness and the promotion of active political involvement" (Held, 1980, p. 22). Lukacs also believed that all social analysis must take into consideration the stages of the preceding historical development and the historical context in which the subject of analysis is found. He also contended that one of the major barriers to revolutionary consciousness is *reification*. In this context, reification is the appearance of peoples' productive activity as something foreign to them (Held, 1980). Reification is a social illusion whereby social phenomena take on the appearance of things. This includes social relationships being reduced to thing-like objects. An example is when the factory worker and his or her products are seen as commodities, as objects. As described by Antonia Darder (1991), "Reification results when transitory historical states of affairs are presented as permanent, natural, and commonsensical, as if they were frozen or fixed in the passage of time" (p. 35). These principles contributed greatly to the work of future critical theorists.

In 1923, the Institute of Social Research, which later came to be known as the Frankfurt School, was founded in Germany. Marxism was the inspirational and theoretical foundation of the Institute. The original director of the Institute was Carl Grunberg, followed by Max Horkheimer in 1929. According to Horkheimer's inaugural address, the members of the Institute were to explore the question of "the interconnection between the economic life of society, the psychic development of the individual, and the transformations in the realm of culture. . . . including not only the so-called spiritual contents of science, art, and religion, but also law, ethics, fashion, public opinion, sport, amusement, life-style, etc." (Horkheimer, 1929, p. 43).

As a result of the rise of the Nazis, the Institute moved to Geneva in 1933 and then to Columbia University, New York, in 1935. Although the terms "critical theory" and "critical theorist" were applied to the research and writing of the members of the Institute, not all associates ascribed devoutly to the philosophy (Held, 1980). Yet most of the members hoped that their work would make a historical contribution as a substantial force in the struggle against domination in all of its forms. Indeed, their work continues to influence the thinking and practice of educators, psychologists, and members of helping fields today.

Critical Theory and Dialectics

According to McLaren (1989), "Critical theorists begin with the premise that *men and women are essentially unfree and inhibit a world rife with contradictions and asymmetries of power and privilege"* (p. 166). Adding to this premise, Tim Dant (1991) offers: "Critical theory questions not just the isolated elements of the society which it takes as its object; it is the whole historical structure which is being criticized. Thus, it questions the values of the existing order of 'better', 'useful', 'appropriate', 'productive' and 'valuable' and is 'wholly distrustful of the rules of conduct which society as presently constituted provides each of its members'" (p. 89). When analyzing an issue from the critical perspective, one uses a *dialectic* method. This method examines the contradictions that are inherent to the subject. Dialectical theory "attempts to tease out the histories and relations of accepted meanings and appearances, tracing out the interactions from the context to the part, from the system inward to the event" (McLaren, 1989, p. 166). From this standpoint, critical theory assists in the focus of both sides of a social contradiction at the same time. According to Antonia Darder (1991), "Dialectical thought seeks out these social contradictions and sets up a process of open and thoughtful questioning that requires reflection to ensure back and forth between the parts and the whole, the object and the subject, knowledge and human action, process and product, so that further contradictions may be discovered" (p. 81). An important point is that the uncovered contradictions need not be bipolar, or opposites. Rather, the elements are complementary and dynamic, not fixed or static. The reevaluation of contradictions leads to new forms of thinking and action which are mandatory in order to go beyond the original position (Darder, 1991).

Power, Knowledge, and Truth

A fundamental characteristic of critical theory is the issue of power and its impact on relationships and the search for truth. The premise that scientific and social research is value-free and neutral, along with a disregard for social relations, especially in terms of culture, resulted from positivist theory (Darder, 1991). French philosopher Michel Foucault's work attempts to shed some light on the socially constructed nature of truth and its impact on knowledge/power relationships (Foucault, 1980). He claims that power is everywhere, at all times. He further claims that the power/knowledge association is intimately embedded in all relationships of domination and resistance (McLaren, 1989).

Critical theorists believe that truth is socially constructed, culturally mediated, and historically positioned. Those discourses, or family of concepts, that are dominant determine what is true, important, and relevant. According to McLaren (1989), "truth cannot be spoken in the absence of power relations, and each relation necessarily speaks its own truth" (p. 181). From a critical standpoint, truth is not absolute and it is not relative; it is relational (Foucault, 1980). That is, statements considered to be "of the truth" are dependent upon history, discipline, institution, culture, and other social factors. These concepts suggest that the search for "the truth" is illusive and fluid. Societies use truths to guide their behavior in the world. If these truths are always changing, then how do we know how to behave in the world? Critical theorists contend that *praxis*, meaning informed actions, must be guided by *phronesis,* or the tendency to act truly and rightly (McLaren, 1989). The promotion of justice and freedom, as well as the elimination of pain, oppression, and inequality, must be the intentness of action and knowledge.

Critical theory holds an important role in the rethinking of social justice and equality in times of diversity. It begins to provide the framework upon which to question societal institutions. This chapter should be considered an introductory lesson in critical theory. The purpose of this chapter has been to begin to create a language and foundation from which to critique traditional counselor education theory and practice. The key concepts identified are as follows:

1. The fundamental theoretical bases from which counselors are trained fail to question links between power and knowledge, and therefore do not confront oppressive elements of practice.

2. Elements of critical theory can assist in this questioning. The main concepts of critical theory which are of greatest use here are the existence of a dominant culture, hegemony, ideology, universal principles, dialectics, and the impact of power on relationships and in defining truth.

3. Through the use of critical theoretical perspectives, the contradictions in everyday life become illumined. Dialectics establish a process of thoughtful reflection and dialogue which work to bring about deeper forms of thinking and action.

Since educational institutions are the main channel through which knowledge flows in a society, several scholars and theorists have applied critical theoretical concepts to education. They began to examine the ways in which schools work to sustain the power and privilege of certain groups, while at the same time oppress, suppress, and repress others. As a result, the notion of critical pedagogy was developed.

4

Critical Pedagogy and Educational Counseling

> The hope is with those who refuse to allow oppression of the mind and the body to become oppression of the spirit and who resist the grotesque identification of education with the economic interests of the dominant class.
>
> —Peter McLaren
> "Schooling the Postmodern Body"
> *Journal of Education*

The application of critical theoretical tenets to education is called *critical pedagogy*. Since our intent is to bring into relation the elements of critical theory with counselor education and practice, the salient aspects of critical pedagogy are most important. A vital step here is the linkage of critical pedagogy with counseling.

In order to facilitate clarity, it is important to decipher the difference between pedagogy and teaching. According to Roger Simon (1987),

Pedagogy is a more complex and extensive term than teaching, referring to the integration in practice of particular curriculum content and design, classroom strategies and techniques, a time and place for the practice of these. . . . and evaluation purpose and methods. All of these aspects of educational practice come together in the realities of what happens in classrooms. Together they organize a view of how teachers' work within an institutional context specifies a particular vision of what knowledge is of most worth, what it means to know something, and how we might construct representations of ourselves, others, and our physical and social environment. In other words, talk about pedagogy is simultaneous talk about details of what students and others might do together and the cultural politics such practice supports. To propose a pedagogy is to propose a political vision. In this perspective, we cannot talk about teaching practices without talking about politics. (p. 371)

CRITICAL PEDAGOGY

Critical educational theory strives to identify and challenge the ways in which schools contribute to the political and cultural life of students (Darder, 1991). Therefore, teachers must understand the role schooling plays in the connection of power and knowledge, and how this either hinders or helps students develop the ability to critically question contradictions and ultimately unite for the purpose of liberation.

Fundamental to the discussion of critical pedagogy is the notion that schooling is a political process. Schools espouse to be value-free and bipartisan. From the critical educator viewpoint, schools maintain a relationship between cultural politics and economic potency in society (Darder, 1991). Upholding the axioms of critical theory, critical pedagogy supports a view of knowledge that is historical and dialectic in nature. Through this perspective, schools become more than places of indoctrination and socilization, but also cultural places that have the ability to foster student empowerment (McLaren, 1989). An example of the contradictions found in education is research which showed that the school functions simultaneously as a means to empower students in terms of imparting notions of social justice and as a means of sustaining, legitimizing, and reproducing dominant class interests. These interests can be found in the creation of obedient, malleable, and low-paid future workers (McLaren, 1989).

Critical educators firmly believe that schools must be partisan. In other words, schools must be committed to a struggle for a qualitative better life for all through the building of a society which rejects all notions of exploitive relationships and excels in social justice. Critical educators believe that schools are not providing the needed guidance for the construction of such a society.

Hegemony

Antonio Gramsci (1971) claims that American educational institutions perpetuate the dominant beliefs, values, and social practices. Darder (1991) explains that "teachers practice hegemony when they fail to teach their students how to question the prevailing social attitudes, values, and social practices of the dominant society in a sustained, critical manner" (p. 88).

Henry Giroux (1983) describes the hegemonic practices in schools by articulating the theory of reproduction. He claims that schools are political players and constantly influence the relationship between "schooling and the workplace, class-specific educational experiences and the job opportunities that emerge for different social groups, the culture of the school and the class-defined culture of the students who attend them, and the relationship among the economic, ideology, and repressive functions of the state and how they affect school policies and practices" (p. 259). Thus, schools are stripped of their political innocence and are connected to the social and cultural matrix of capitalist rationality. In light of reproductive theory, the liberal view of education as the equalizer must be challenged. As Paul Willis (1983) states,

Education was not about equality, but inequality. Education's main purpose of the social integration of a class society could be achieved only by preparing most kids for an unequal future, and by insuring their personal underdevelopment. Far from productive roles in the economy simply waiting to be "fairly" filled by the products of education, the "reproduction" perspective reverses this to suggest that capitalist production and its roles required certain educational outcomes. (p. 110)

According to Giroux (1983), schools are seen as reproductive in three senses: (1) they provide different classes and social groups with the knowledge and skills they need to occupy their respective places in a labor force stratified by class, race, and gender; (2) they are seen as reproductive in the cultural sense, functioning in part to distribute and legitimate forms of knowledge, values, language, and modes of behavior that constitute the dominate culture and its interests; and (3) schools are viewed as part of the government apparatus that produce and legitimate the economical and ideological imperatives that support political power. By appearing to be an impartial and neutral "transmitter" of the benefits of a valued culture, schools are able to promote inequality in the name of objectivity and fairness. Thus, educational institutions exhibit major contradictions between objectivity and neutrality, between dominant ideology and the daily lived experiences of students, and between being an equalizing societal force and "imposing a definition of the social world that is consistent with its interests" (Bourdieu, 1979, p. 30).

Another element of the school's hegemonic function is that of cultural invasion. This "represents an antidialogical action that serves in the sustained social, political, and economic oppression of the subordinate groups" (Darder, 1991, p. 36). Cultural invasion is an act of disrespect, imposition, and domination; there exists a clear relationship between culture and power. According to Paulo Freire (1970), all forms of domination involve some element of invasion. When cultural invasion is cloaked in hegemonic educational practices, the dynamics of a "hidden curriculum" are at work (Bowles & Gintis, 1977). Therefore, educators need to be aware and critical of the subtle ways in which a prescribed curriculum reinforces the values, beliefs, and customs of the dominant society while at the same time silences and oppresses all other ideologies.

Resistance Theory

As was discussed previously, it may appear as though the power of hegemonic, reproductive practice is omnipotent and those of the subordinate groups are forever at the mercy of domination. This is not the case. Two factors support this belief. First, the Marxist theory of contradiction contends that each social group contains within it the seeds of its own destruction and transcendence. All oppressed groups have the ability to recognize when they are being exploited, create a united consciousness, and fight for liberation. Second, hegemony must be reinforced constantly in order to be preserved. According to Darder (1991), "[hegemony] is not something that simply consists of the projection of the ideas of the dominant classes into the heads of the subordinate classes. The footing on which hegemony moves and functions has to shift ground constantly in order to accommodate the changing nature of historical circumstances and the complex demands and critical actions of human beings" (p. 42). The burden to maintain the results of hegemonic practice rests on the dominant culture. Within the hegemonic process, established meanings often are tinged with contradiction and ambiguity. According to resistance theory, human beings not only have the acute ability to challenge the contradictions between what is dictated in the schools and what they know as their realities of everyday life, but they also possess the ability to critically and dialectically engage these contradictions. According to Giroux (1983), "human behavior is rooted in a complex nexus of structured needs, common sense, and critical consciousness, and that ideology is located in all of these aspects of human behavior and thought so as to produce multiple subjectivities and perceptions of the world and everyday life" (p. 18). Further, Darder (1991) contends that, "despite this hegemonic control, members of subordinate and oppressed cultures continue to resist in an effort to struggle for power and control over their own lives" (p. 43). Critical educators hold fast to the belief in their students' abilities to question in a dialectical manner, to identify the contradictions between what is taught in school and what their lives are about, and to join together for the purpose of liberation.

The battle of oppressed groups to obtain and maintain elements of control over their lives is well documented in history. Paradoxically, the early settlers of America were resisting oppressive religious doctrine by leaving their homelands. When African American slaves started to secretly educate their children, they were acting out of resistance in the face of oppressive "rules" that did not allow for slaves to learn to read and write. As with oppressive practices, the goal is to maintain culture and power in the hands of the dominate group. During the much controversial Vietnam War, thousands of young men resisted the call to duty by burning draft cards and fleeing to the safety of the Canadian borders. A more recent example of resistant behavior is the 1991 civil unrest in the streets of Los Angeles. For many, the community destruction was an act of resistance due to years of oppression and lack of power and equality. Historical events are not always ruled by those in power. In fact, "history is, on the contrary, a continuous struggle of individuals and groups to change what exists in each given moment. But for the struggle to be effective, these individuals and groups must feel superior to what exists, and capable of educating society" (Bates, 1975, p. 365).

The concept of resistance is evolving as part of educational theory. The past theoretical neglect of the inclusion of resistance can be traced to the failings of both conservative and radical approaches to schooling. As explained by Giroux (1983), "Conservative educators analyze oppositional behavior primarily through psychological categories that serve to define such behavior not only as deviant, but, more importantly, as destructive and inferior—a failing on the part of the individuals and social groups that exhibit it" (p. 282). On the other hand, radical educators posit discourse focusing on the notion of domination, class conflict, and hegemony while disregarding how teachers, students, and others live out their daily lives in schools. There has been little regard for how human agency accommodates, mediates, and resists the logic of power and the dominating social practices that result.

Educational theories of resistance rely on an understanding of the complexities of culture to define the relationship between schools and the dominant society (McLaren, 1989). Resistant theorists challenge the school's illusory role as a democratic institution that functions to improve the social position of all students—including those groups that are subordinated to the system. As long as school systems continue to misappropriate funds by allocating more monies to the most capable students' activities and more affluent schools, as long as the students continue to be "tracked" according to their ability to achieve by the dominant societies' standards, and as long as students are not allowed to engage in critical dialectical discourse that challenges the contradictions of their daily lives, then the illusion of democratic practices in the schools will continue. The counterpart of such hegemonic practices is resistance.

Individual acts of resistance may lack overt political project and often reflect social practices that are informal and atheoretical in nature. There exists a *range* of oppositional behaviors, some of which constitute resistance and some of which do not. In other words, not all oppositional behavior has "radical significance," nor is all such behavior a clear-cut response to domination. Therefore, it is important to critically evaluate supposed acts of resistance in order to decipher actual counteraction. The issue here is the need to "understand how subordinate groups embody and express a combination of reactionary and progressive behaviors—behaviors that embody ideologies both underlying the structure of social domination and containing the logic necessary to overcome it" (Giroux, 1983, p. 284).

A major contribution to resistance theory has been the discovery by British researcher Willis. His study suggests that working-class students who engage in classroom behaviors of resistance often implicate themselves even further into their own domination (McLaren, 1989). This group of working-class boys, known as "the lads," favored masculine manual labor (reflecting the shop floor culture of their families) as an act of resistance against the class-based oppression of the schools. By this act, they ironically bypassed the school's potential to help them escape the shop floor once they graduated. Thus, these young men not only discarded the alleged superiority of mental labor, they also rejected its underlying ideology that respect and obedience would be exchanged for knowledge and success. As described by Giroux (1983), "The lads oppose this ideology because the counter-logic embodied in the families, workplaces, and street life that make up *their* culture points to a different and more convincing reality. Thus, one major contribution that has emerged from resistance studies is the insight that the mechanisms of reproduction are never complete and are always faced with partially realized elements of opposition" (p. 282). By rejecting schooling, the lads discounted the power of critical thinking as a tool of social transformation. In other words, resistance is transformative only when students begin to use the knowledge to help empower themselves and others toward social reform.

In another study of student resistance, similar logic was displayed by dropouts from alternative schools in New York City's South Bronx (Fine, 1982). The researcher assumed that the students who dropped out of these schools were victims of "learned helplessness," but she discovered instead that they were the most critical and politically astute students in the alternative schools: "Much to our collective surprise (and dismay) the dropouts were those students who were most likely to identify injustice in their social lives and at school, and most ready to correct injustice by criticizing or challenging a teacher. The dropouts were least depressed and had attained academic levels equivalent to students who remained in school" (Fine, 1982, p. 6). While such students were capable of challenging the dominant ideology of the school, they failed to recognize the limits of their own resistance. The irony here is that by leaving school, they cut themselves off from the political and social avenues conducive to change and social justice.

As has been suggested, resistant student behavior takes on many forms. Not all students who are able to see through the lies and promises of the dominant school ideology translate this insight into overt rebellious behavior. More subtle, yet as important, forms of resistance may be withdrawal from the classroom activities, frequent absenteeism, or a hesitation to accept the hegemonic curriculum presented. These students may believe that overt rebelliousness may result in powerlessness now and in the future. Some of these students may stay and complete school, but on their own terms. Their future may be one of limited opportunities. Giroux (1983) explains, "but what is of major importance here is that any other alternative seems ideologically naive and limits whatever transcendent hope for the future these students may have" (p. 289).

Resistance theory redefines the causes and meanings of oppositional behavior by arguing that it may have little to do with deviance and learned helplessness. Rather, resistant behavior has a great deal to do with moral and political indignation. It is imperative that educators and counselors become aware of what constitutes resistance and what does not, and be more specific about how the concept of resistance can be used to develop a more critical pedagogy. There is a call for resistance to be grounded in a theoretical rationale that provides a framework for the examination of schools as social sites which structure the experiences of subordinate groups.

The concept of resistance not only shifts the theoretical ground for analyzing oppositional behavior, but it also identifies the need to examine student concerns which are generally neglected in the traditional views of schooling. An essential aspect of critical pedagogy centers around the need for students to interrogate critically their inner histories and experiences. It is crucial for students to be able to understand how their own experiences are reinforced, contradicted, and suppressed as a result of the hegemonic materials and intellectual practices that characterize daily classroom life. McLaren (1989) claims, "to resist means to fight against the monitoring of passion and desire" (p. 188). This philosophical approach to the analysis of oppositional behaviors may serve educators and students as well. All forms of oppositional behavior should be critically analyzed in order to determine if emancipatory interests are at work (Giroux, 1983).

Most often teachers, administrators, and counselors view students' oppositional behavior as counterproductive, uncooperative, and problematic. The focus is put on making the child behave and get along in the classroom. The primary goal is to get all of the students to be obedient, well mannered, orderly, quiet, on-task, and easily manageable. By reframing oppositional behavior in terms of resistance theory, one recognizes that student resistance in all forms represents manifestations of struggle and solidarity that challenge and confirm capitalist hegemony. According to Giroux (1983), "what is most important is the willingness of radical educators to search for the emancipatory interests that underlie such resistance and to make them visible to students and others so that they can become the object of debate and political analysis" (p. 293).

Historicity of Knowledge

The notion of the historicity of knowledge, as developed by the Frankfurt School, is an important characteristic of critical pedagogy. The historical realities and the social practices of schools must be examined together (Darder, 1991). Education grounded in critical theory demands that the study of history be raised to a level of critical examination and exploration. Instead of passively accepting the stories of this country's founding fathers, students need to understand history as a social process. This means that the mediating factors which make up history, including economics, social movements, government politics, and cultural forces, also must be taught and critiqued.

Educational allegiance to the dominant school culture upholds and perpetuates the political, economic, and social causes of the dominant society. This tunnel focus works to marginalize and nullify other sources of knowledge, mainly, that which originates from oppressed and subordinate groups. As long as the main thrust of school curricula is toward the contributions, lives, and stories of white men, while at the same time ignoring the contributions, lives, and stories of people of color, women, and the working class, liberation and social justice will allude our society (Darder, 1991).

Dialectical Theory, Praxis, and Education

In upholding the philosophical foundations of critical theory, critical pedagogy adheres to dialectical theory. The dialectical approach of critical educators encompasses a process that assists the students in questioning the contradictions found between their daily lived experiences and that which is taught in school. According to Darder (1991), "A dialectical view begins with the fact of human existence and the contradictions and disjunctions that, in part, shape it and make problematic its meaning in the world. It functions to assist students to analyze their world, to become aware of the limitations that prevent them from changing the world, and, finally, to help them collectively struggle to transform that world" (p. 81).

As has been stated, the dialectical process searches for social contradictions through critical questioning and reflecting. The quest is not to set up dichotomous elements, but rather to invoke a process to further understand the deficiencies in the social structure. The desired outcome is the formulation of new creative ways of thinking and acting which eventually will bring about group unity and liberation. According to Darder (1991), "the ultimate purpose of a dialectical critique is critical thinking in the interest of social change" (p. 82).

This new thinking, reflection, and action formulate what critical educators call *praxis*. Praxis is "self-creating and self-generating free human action" (Darder, 1991, p. 83). It is the union of theory and practice. Critical educators contend that without theory, practice fails to create justice and equality. Praxis is not the teaching of theory for the purpose of action. Rather, it is the students' participation in the discovery of critical theory, the dialectical process, critique, and the resulting commitment to change (Giroux, 1983). Students are seen as active agents with the ability and depth to comprehend, question, decipher meaning, and collectively act on their own world, producing change that transforms their realities.

Discourse

Students must feel accepted and validated in order to fully participate in a critical pedagogical environment. The reality of oppressed persons is that even if they rise above the hegemonic forces within society, their voice is most often not heard. There is a dominant discourse which is louder than the subordinate groups' pleas. This sadly works to silence women, people of color, and other oppressed groups. Thus, there is a power dynamic that is always functioning. Critical pedagogy encourages a critical discourse that attempts to shift the power from dominant discourse and authority to a discourse that represents the subordinate reality. The discursive rules and practices, such as who can speak and when, and who must listen and why, are challenged and changed through critical discourse.

Language is the primary vehicle through which our subjective experiences are shaped (McLaren, 1988). Critical educators believe that it is through the language of the dominant culture that knowledge is imparted and validated. Thus, truth is relational, that is, based on relations of power within a society (Foucault, 1980). A major goal of critical discourse is to challenge and question the dominant discourse with immediacy, the moment of hegemonic accent. Practiced in this way, critical discourse becomes a transformative act (Darder, 1991).

Dialogue is a reciprocal process—one in which the teacher learns from the students and the students learn from the teacher. Classroom dialogue takes on a historical perspective that includes the day-to-day realities of the student. Students are active agents in the learning process (Darder, 1991). They are encouraged to question the ways in which they have become what and who they are, as well as how they could change. According to Darder (1991), "In this way, critical educators encourage the free and uncoerced exchange of ideas and experiences. They demonstrate a caring for their students and provide them with emotional support to help them overcome their feelings of inadequacy and guilt as they become critics of the world they inhabit" (p. 95). The dialogue method helps the student to change their self-perception from that of near helpless (most often unaware of the dominant societal influence) to that of social transformation agent. It is by way of praxis, the joining of reflective thought and action, that a deepening awareness is brought about.

Critical pedagogy is committed to the freedom of students to act on their world through the development of their critical consciousness. This is called the process of *conscientization*. It is the process whereby students move from being "recipients of knowledge, but as knowing subjects" (Darder, 1991, p. 95). Students develop an intense awareness of how their lives have been shaped by sociopolitical and economic forces. It is from this awareness that students then explore their personal and collective powers to change these forces. As students strip away the social myths that have molded their realities, they also strip away their imposed disempowerment.

CRITICAL PEDAGOGY AS A FOUNDATION FOR COUNSELING

Since critical theory is not within the realm of traditional educational discourse, students in counseling preparation may find the concepts foreign and in direct opposition to the dominant ideology that they have embraced all their lives. Consequently, some students will resist, while others will "stay at the table" through the struggle of dealing with difference. And still others will experience validation of their own experiences of subordination and thus feel safer to speak and hopefully have their voices heard. At times this can be extremely disconcerting and uncomfortable for those counselor educators who need the learning experience to be solely under their control and the classroom to be a peaceful place.

As was just discussed, much has been written about the dimensions of critical education and the development of critical educators (Darder, 1991; Giroux, 1981, 1988a, b; McLaren, 1988). There is, however, minimal representation of critical counseling or the development of critical counselors in the literature. Since a main focus of this book is a critique of educational counseling and the preparation of counselors, the elements of critical pedagogy are most applicable. Through the utilization of critical pedagogy, a new foundation for counselor education begins to emerge. An examination of counseling practices in terms of the eight characteristics of critical theory (Darder, 1991) is a beginning point for building a critical platform of analysis. Therefore, I will use the following characteristics as a framework of critique: (1) cultural politics; (2) economics; (3) history of knowledge; (4) dialectical view of world/knowledge; (5) theory of ideology and hegemony; (6) resistance; (7) development of consciousness; and (8) praxis.

Cultural Politics

According to Darder (1991), "fundamental to critical pedagogy is the assumption that teachers must understand the role schooling plays in uniting knowledge and power, how this dynamic relates to the development of critical thinking and socially active lives" (p. 77). Therefore, the traditional belief that schools are neutral and apolitical in nature is unacceptable and false. A critical educator, or counselor, undoubtedly must associate any theory of education with power, politics, history, and culture. The exposure and challenge of the roles schools play in the political and cultural life of students is, therefore, a major impetus of a critical approach.

Schools wield tremendous power and control over the definition and legitimization of what is considered knowledge and what is considered success. Traditionally, the role of the counselor is to assist the teacher, via intervention, with children who display disruptive behaviors or emotions in the classroom. Counselors help the child adjust, behave, succeed, and adapt according to the dominant society's definition and meaning of what is normal and acceptable.

Counselors ultimately possess positions of great power and authority over students. This power and control reveals itself in counseling practices in several different ways. For example, decisions regarding a student's future career path often rely on a counselor's opinion regarding college preparatory classes or vocational training. Unfortunately, these decisions are not always made from a substantiated position. The reliance upon stereotypic cultural perceptions, personal biases, and a failure to appreciate a student's lived experiences effectively result in erroneous assumptions about a student's abilities, goals, desires, and life-style. Because counselors are not adequately trained in multicultural issues, they unwittingly perpetuate their own prejudicial biases and stereotypic beliefs. In fact, much of the oppressive behaviors of counselors go unrecognized by themselves, students, parents, and administrators.

Counselors exert a certain power over the definition of acceptable behavior, feelings, and attitudes. An example of such power is the perpetuation of values embraced by the dominant society. Individualism, autonomous decision making, monetary gain, cooperation, and status are some of the values rewarded by the Euro–North American culture. Counselors routinely present classroom guidance lessons on "proper" ways to deal with anger, grief, conflict, and intimacy. The teaching and support of particular life-styles and communication styles send out very clear messages regarding what is "right" and what is "wrong"; unquestionably, that which mirrors the dominant society is always labeled "right."

Economics

A popular but naive assumption exists that American schools function based on individual and social empowerment. When viewed from a critical perspective, however, it is clear that, often, the exact opposite is true. The students in the most need of these individual and social opportunities typically attend schools with the least financial support. The consequences of this are significant with respect to those in power maintaining their position and perpetuating the status quo. Students attending schools with limited financial support receive fewer chances for empowerment. For example, schools presiding in economically impoverished communities must cut student services and activities due to budgetary restraints. Additionally, counseling services are often among those eliminated. However, perhaps no counseling is better than oppressive counseling practices.

Success in school can be achieved only through the adoption of the dominant versions of truth and knowledge. According to Darder (1991),

Those who succeed are considered to possess the individual merits that consequently also make them privilege to the economic goods that success can bring in the United States. Those who fail are considered to lack the individual intelligence, maturity, or drive to succeed. Seldom acknowledged in this traditional analysis of student success or failure are the asymmetrical power relations determined by cultural and economic forces that grant privileges to students from the dominant culture. (p. 78)

As was previously mentioned, counselors can control and dominate students' economic futures through counseling and guidance practices. It is well documented that counselors tend to encourage and push the motivated, bright, and middle-to upper-class students toward college and discourage or even ignore minority students' career development (Hawks & Muha, 1991). Essentially, counselors deprive minority students, as a whole, of the attention and encouragement essential for success. As a result, counselors unknowingly maintain a supply of unskilled persons to occupy lower paying jobs in the marketplace. Unfortunately, this labor force is largely composed of the minority groups so often denied adequate attention and support.

History of Knowledge

Critical educators assist students in the understanding of the interconnection between history and social process. Traditionally, school curricula and counselor education programs blatantly ignored the histories of women, people of color, and the working class. Thus, curricula "marginalize and invalidate knowledge forms and experiences that are significant to subordinate and oppressed groups" (Darder, 1991, p. 79). Counselor training and practices long have been described as culturally encapsulated (Wrenn, 1962), ignoring the historical continuities and historical development of any group other than the dominant group.

Until recently, the dogma perpetuated by traditional theory and practice was unchallenged; there was no recognition, exploration, or validation of any other cultural view of human development, personality, behavior, attitudes, feelings, experiences, or values. Recognition and an exploration of the students' own histories and systems of meaning, therefore, remained minimal. The development of self-empowerment is best assisted and nurtured when individuals' life experiences and interpretations are acknowledged and appreciated. Counseling is performed in a vacuum state when the students' personal histories are not an element of consideration.

Dialectical Theory

Traditional theories of education and counseling function on the technical control of both knowledge and power. A critical educator or counselor provides students with a form of engagement that allows them to fully examine the underlying, hidden political, social, and economic contexts in which they live. The purpose of this type of exchange is to uncover the social contradictions experienced in everyday life, construct new forms of thinking, and empower the group to take political action in order to transcend oppression.

Counseling practices traditionally encourage self-exploration and challenge, yet this exploration is monitored in order to control the degree of tension that may result. Therefore, self-exploration never reaches a point of critical review of the students' worlds and realities. For example, counselors do not support student discussions which analyze and link the contradictions of their individual lives and relationships to the social dimensions of class, gender, race, and sexual orientation. Since an outcome of this type of dialectical practice is reclaiming the conditions of self-determined existence (Darder, 1991), and since a desired goal of counseling is ideally congruent with this concept, counselors must begin to examine a more dialectical approach with students.

Theory of Ideology and Hegemony

Ideology is the framework of thought used by a society to give order and meaning to the social and political world. Hegemony is a term used to describe the process of social control through which the dominant ideology, world view and social practices are upheld. According to Darder (1991), "The dominant society does not need to impose hegemony by force, since the oppressed actively subscribe to many of the values and objectives of the dominant class without being aware of the source of those values or interests that inform them" (p. 87). In essence, hegemonic practices result in the domination of women, members of the working class, and people of color.

Critical educators and counselors recognize hegemony and constantly teach students to question the prevailing social attitudes, values, and social practices of the dominant society. Yet, too often, counselors function from a place of unexamined assumptions, particularly their own, concerning who is in power and why, and assumptions regarding cultural, gender, race, class, age, and sexual orientation differences. Unfortunately, most counselors have yet to question how hegemony has influenced their own lives, let alone the lives of their clients and students.

Resistance

Human beings possess an undeniable potential to challenge the contradictions existent between the theories and beliefs dictated in the schools and the realities of everyday life. In addition, they also possess the ability to critically and dialectically engage in these contradictions. Hegemonic practices are countered by what is referred to as *resistance*. Resistance can be defined as: "a personal space, in which the logic and force of domination is contested by the power of subjective agency to subvert the process of socialization. Seen this way, resistance functions as a type of negation or affirmation placed before ruling discourses and practices" (Giroux, 1988b, p. 162). All persons have the ability to make meaning of their lives and to resist oppression.

Those who ignore the resistant theory often misinterpret oppositional student behavior as delinquent, troubled, emotionally unstable, at risk, deprived, disadvantaged, uncontrollable, and difficult. In addition, teachers, administrators, and counselors view students' oppositional behavior as counterproductive, uncooperative, and problematic. The focus then becomes that of making the child behave and get along in the classroom. Admittedly, however, not all oppositional behavior is an act of resistance against hegemony. A critical counselor is well versed in resistance theory and is able to recognize when student resistance actually represents manifestations of struggle and solidarity that challenge and confront capitalist hegemony. It is through acts of resistance that hope for liberation and social justice continues to thrive.

Counselors, because of their influential role, possess the power and the opportunity to assist students in uncovering their emancipatory interests and to support liberatory acts.

Development of a Social Consciousness

Critical theorists support the notion that through the sharing and critique of their life experiences, students will begin to discover themselves as social agents with powers to resist overt and covert oppressive forces. As a result of critical questioning and discussions, students move toward a deeper awareness of the economic and sociopolitical realities that influence their lives. This process helps students in the transformation of apathetic attitudes and behaviors. Expression and validation of life experiences and frustrations create a sense of group unity, solidarity, and identity. From this place of solidarity, transformative political action can take place.

There exists an individualistic approach to counseling. That is to say, importance is placed on *individual* achievement, development, and needs, as opposed to *group* or *community* achievement, development, and needs. Due to this individualistic approach to counseling, often, separation from "the group" is encouraged and group solidarity for political action is discouraged. This separation reduces the students' abilities to develop and strengthen collective identity and the consciousness needed for a deepening awareness of the sociopolitical and economic realities that shape their lives and their capacities to recreate these realities. Even though counselors believe that they are helping students to create a better life, this "better life" is not one that has been created as a result of critical thinking; rather, it is created from a hegemonic ideological framework.

Paulo Freire (1970) coined the term *conscientization,* which means a consciousness of self in relation to contextual and cultural issues. The focus is on the liberation of a person from personal, social, and economic oppression. This cultural awareness should be a goal of education and, therefore, counselor education as well. In a counseling setting, clients may blame themselves for their conditions and major circumstances. Counselors need to be skilled at liberating these clients from self-blame and encourage them to see their issues in a social context. What follows then, is the facilitation of personal action to improve the condition (Ivey, Ivey, & Simek-Morgan, 1993).

Praxis

Praxis is known as self-creating and self-generating human action (Darder, 1991). Humans have the innate ability to critically evaluate their lives and to take creative movement toward liberation from any oppressive conditions. Therefore, all human activity consists of action and reflection, or praxis. The three required elements of praxis are theory, practice, and critique. Freire (1985) contends that true praxis is impossible in the undialectical vacuum where we are driven by a subject/object dichotomy. Theory and practice lose their power to transform reality when such a dichotomy exists.

Counselors tend to reduce students to objects when they practice behavioral strategies and techniques. In this context, students are viewed as controllable "things" instead of beings with the capacity to think, evaluate, and act on behalf of their own liberation. In order for praxis to occur, students must be viewed and treated as cognitive subjects who are able to "accept their concrete situation as a challenging condition—that they are able to change its meaning by their action" (Darder, 1991, p. 84).

Until critical theory is applied to counseling training, theory, and practices, the intent to transform inequity remains limited. Counselors must be willing to critically evaluate the interchange and outcomes of the theories and practices that they employ. The litmus test should be the degree to which students are free to question and change the status quo.

Ideally, education and counseling should be transformative activities that create conditions of empowerment via a central concern for social justice and democracy. Educators and counselors have become dependent upon structured, proven methods of teaching and counseling. Unlike prescribed lesson plans and traditional counseling techniques, critical approaches do not enlist specific techniques; there is no recipe. Critical counselors must, therefore, develop the ability and comfort to question, resist, and change their own lives and communities before they can model this process of empowerment for students.

While the counseling profession has made progress in terms of multicultural awareness, it has a long way to go with respect to incorporating critical theory in counselor training and practice. Counselors and counselor educators need to unify with others who expound and live critical theory. Ultimately, the struggle is for a qualitative better life for all. To ensure this goal and actually achieve social justice, counselors must develop and operate from a critical agenda. In other words, we must critically "clean house" and explore ways in which we participate in the subordination of groups through hegemonic values, beliefs, and practices.

The purpose of this chapter has been to offer an expanded language and foundation from which we may critique traditional counselor education theory and practice. Two key concepts identified are as follows:

1. Because the focus of critique is educational counseling, the elements of critical pedagogy are most applicable. Through the utilization of the eight characteristics of critical pedagogy, a new foundation for counselor education begins to emerge.

2. At this point of exploration, it is understood that due to traditional counselor education:
    —counselors hold power to perpetuate values embraced by the dominant society;
    —counselors can control and dominate students' economic futures through guid-

ance and counseling practices;

—counseling is performed in a vacuum state when the students' personal histories are not an element of consideration;

—by not using a dialectical approach, counselors fail to encourage student discussions that analyze and link the contradictions of their individual lives and relationships to the social dimensions of class, gender, race, and sexual orientation;

—counselors often function from a place of unexamined assumptions;

—counselors fail to see oppositional student behavior as possible resistance;

—counselors are not skilled at liberating clients from self-blame, nor do they encourage clients to see their issues in a social context;

—without the infusion of critical theory into counselor education, counselors will most likely perpetuate oppressive and exclusionary practices that fail to question the status quo.

An additional and vital component of counselor education's agenda for a critical pedagogy is the application of critical theoretical suppositions to traditional psychology. As was identified in the discussion about multiculturalism, traditional psychology is embraced as a major construct within educational counseling. Through the process of deconstructing exclusionary and oppressive aspects of mainstream psychological ideologies, another facet of critical educational counseling emerges.

5

A Critical Psychology: Deepening the Understanding of Critical Counselor Education

> We can theoretically reach further than our empirical research can go, in the hope that our theoretical reach can help us to extend our practical grasp.
>
> —Robert Laing
> *Going Crazy*

A psychology that embraces a commitment to social justice and the purpose of liberatory practice is a critical psychology. A critical psychology uncovers the contradictions between the beliefs, values, and customs of the ascendant culture and the daily lived experiences of oppressed groups. Critical psychologists question the relevance of psychological theory and practice. They contend that what has been labeled as mainstream "bourgeois" psychology is based on the ideology and interests of a dominant culture, thus having limited relevance to the interests of the working class. A critical psychology attempts to overcome abstractness and isolation and to bring about a concreteness to human nature. People are seen in *relation*; that is, in a societal and historical context. According to Tolman and Maiers (1991), "Critical psychology seeks to become a psychology that is not merely *about* people but a psychology that is *for* people" (p. 22).

This chapter will identify and discuss the characteristics of a critical psychology. Advancing these ideas further, feminist theory offers ways of analyzing unequal power relationships and oppressive gender roles. Feminist psychology, which is feminist theory applied to psychology, provides new perspectives for counseling in a world in which the power lines are shifting. Also included in this chapter is how these concepts enhance a critical pedagogy of counselor education.

CRITICAL PSYCHOLOGY: AN OVERVIEW

Critical psychology began as a political protest against traditional psychology, claiming that it had aligned itself with one segment of the population against another, that being the dominant class against the subordinate class. Early critical psychologists and theorists held fast to the belief that it was possible to organize scientifically, theoretically, and politically a psychology that addressed and served the interests of the working class (Tolman & Maiers, 1991). This strong political emphasis set apart this protest from others, such as behaviorism and Gestalt psychology. Unlike other protests, this one successfully showed how political issues are translated into theoretical and methodological terms, most of which are familiar.

A fundamental premise for all critical theoretical approaches is the idea that there is no absolute truth. In other words, the bottom line of undeniable certainty will never be reached. This causes great anxiety with those wanting and needing black-and-white answers, security, and tidy theories of the nature of human behavior. Those who feel the most discomfort are those who count on psychological theory to manipulate, control, and second guess the behaviors of others. Control-based institutions such as business, government, military, and schools desperately cling to the traditional ways of interpreting psychological concepts.

A critical psychology uncovers the previously concealed power dynamics that operate within a society. The ultimate desired intention is to broaden the scope of personal freedom for all of the members of society. This type of psychology would interpret human behavior in such a way as to enable men, women, and children to understand what is happening in their world in the context of their social structures (Sullivan, 1990). For example, the student who is experiencing failure in a subject will not fall into the automatic trap that failure in school is simply the result of lack of individual motivation. Examination of the educational setting and institutional structure also would be considerations when looking at the student's inability to achieve a passing mark.

Of great importance to a critical approach to psychology is the notion that the mode of inquiry is value-full, as opposed to the value-free concept of conventional theory. For the critical theorist, there are no pretensions of being value-free, and, in fact, the values surrounding all types of human liberation from oppressive experiences are openly advocated. According to Edmund Sullivan (1990), "the task of a critical psychology is to identify the hegemonic structural factors in the organization of our society which create systematic oppression for specific cultural groups" (p. 91). Sullivan uses Antonio Gramsci's definition of hegemony, which refers to a form of ideological control in which dominant social practices, beliefs, and values are reproduced and disseminated through a range of institutions such as schools, family, and mass media. Here, the emphasis is on the reality of domination. According to critical thinkers, there exists, at any particular time, a central system of practices, meanings, and values that is unmistakenly interpreted as dominant and powerful. Clearly stated,

It is a whole body of practices and expectations; our assignments of energy, our ordinary understanding of the nature of man and of his world. It is a set of meanings and values which as they are experienced as practices appear as reciprocally confirming. It thus constitutes a sense of reality for most people in the society, a sense of the absolute because experienced as reality beyond which it is difficult for most members of the society to move, in most areas of their lives. (Williams, 1973, p. 205)

The notion that the study of human behavior is never value-free or nonpartisan is a radical scientific concept because the more "scientific"—meaning value-free and nonpartisan—the research is, the more believable and acceptable the results. This is the mythical aspect of research. According to Charles Tolman (in Tolman & Maiers, 1991), "Science is a societal practice and has to do with societal existence; as such, it cannot be value-free. Its very existence presupposes its societal value. The point of critical psychology's partisanship is to make its societal value as conscious as possible. This partisanship can be expressed in class terms: It takes the side of the working classes. But more important, it takes the side of the individual human subject" (p. 5). Critical psychology insists that there is a social embeddedness of social science. Because of this embeddedness, the concepts of organized science, theory, and method will be blindly reproduced (Tolman & Maiers, 1991).

From a critical stance, psychology must be partisan, that is, for the individual human agent. If it is nonpartisan, then only the interests of the dominant culture are examined, resulting in findings that are relevant to one sector of the population. According to Tolman and Maiers (1991), "a psychology that deals with averages in the hopes of achieving generality through abstraction can never become relevant to the particular individual" (p. 5). Critical psychologists believe that by the insistence on the measurement and statistical use of dependent and independent variables, the capitalists' need to control and manipulate the masses is accomplished. As this occurs, the focus on the experience or problems of the individuals becomes lost.

Those who conduct psychological experiments believe that the outcome of the experiments is some kind of disinterested rationality. Critical theory questions this idea with the approach that all experiments are a reflection of certain cultural rationalities based on technical control (Habermas, 1972). According to Edmund Sullivan (1984), "knowledge is based on a particular *interest* reflected in modern scientific society, and this knowledge-constitutive interest (i.e., technical-control rationality) shapes what counts as knowledge" (p. 5). Therefore, psychological research findings may well mask the political intentions of those in power.

A critical psychology changes the language of psychology, from a language of hidden manipulation to a language of emancipation. According to Sullivan (1990), "A critical psychology, like all social inquiry with emancipatory impulses, should embrace the task of searching for the new social relations and the new social conflicts that form themselves in a profoundly transformed cultural field" (p. 108). In other words, a critical psychology interprets human behaviors in ways and with ideologies that are anti-hegemonic in nature. This is not to say that we throw the baby out with the bath water and disavow orthodox psychological theory and practice. Rather, we rethink and reevaluate those concepts which reify human nature and perpetuate human suffering and inequities.

A Critical Psychology Metaphor: The Personal

As was discussed in Chapter 2, there are two metaphors used in conventional, traditional psychology: mechanical and organic. Mechanical metaphors are based on the assumption of analysis: The whole is the sum of its parts. Structuralism and other organic metaphors are premised on the principle of synthesis: The whole is more than the sum of its parts. Proponents of a critical psychology have introduced and applied a third metaphor for the understanding of the human world, the *personal metaphor*. By way of introduction of the personal metaphor:

We are not organisms, but persons. The nexus of relations which unites us in a human society is not organic but personal. Human behavior cannot be understood, but only caricatured, if it is represented as an adaptation to environment; and there is no such process as social evolution but, instead, a history which reveals a precarious development and possibilities both of progress and of retrogression—the personal necessarily includes an organic aspect—and this organic aspect is continuously qualified by its conclusion, so that it cannot even be properly abstracted, except through a prior understanding of the personal structure in which it is an essential, though subordinate component. A descent from the personal is possible, in theory, and indeed in practice; but there is no way to ascend from the organic to the personal. The organic of man [woman] excludes, by its very nature, all the characteristics in virtue of which we are human beings. To include them we must change our categories afresh from the beginning. (MacMurray, 1961, pp. 46–47)

This is not to imply that there is no value in mechanical and organic metaphors, rather, that their use should be restricted and perhaps a more appropriate metaphor encouraged.

The personal metaphor is a relational metaphor. That is, in order to understand human nature, one must develop some sort of systematic interpretation of the communication expressions in relational contexts (Sullivan, 1990). "The individual, before it can determine itself, is determined by the relations in which it is enmeshed. It is a fellow-being before it's a being" (Jacoby, 1975, p. 34). The fundamental relational quality of this metaphor is based on "persons in relation" (MacMurray, 1957).

The primary unit of analysis is the person or the individual. Yet this does not exclude the larger social structure, for example, class, gender, and ethnicity. The interpretation of the individual is not individualistic or egocentric in nature (Sampson, 1981). According to Sullivan (1990),

We are assuming that the individual expressions or symbols are for purposes of communication; therefore, the unit of analysis must be a "you and I" rather than an isolated "I." Our assumption is that individuals use expressions because they intend meanings for others. Expressions are *ambiguous* because the meaning or significance of expression is contingent upon multiple actors communicating with one another. Humans, it would appear, are peculiar animals involved in webs of significance that they themselves have spun. (p. 19)

Thus, meaning can be multiple and ambiguous, which seeks interpretation. A person's culture may be said to be a "web of significance" (Geertz, 1973). With the emerging recognition of culture as a powerful force in a person's psychological life (Fernando, 1988, 1991; Segall, Dansan, Berry, & Poortinga, 1990; Smith, 1985; Sue, 1973; White, 1984), the exploration and interpretation of this "web" is essential. Human cultural expressions are intricate and complex in nature. Due to this, interpreting meaning will not be adequately accomplished with a scientific experimental search for laws. What is required is a self-reflective interpretive search for meaning (Geertz, 1973).

According to Sullivan (1990), "the personal world is the cultural world; culture is the womb in which personhood grows and transforms" (p. 24). It is important to note that growth in this context does not mean a type of organic development or metaphor. Sullivan (1990) goes on to explain:

When one speaks of personal growth, that is saying that the personal world is cultivated within cultural forms. By cultural forms, I mean specified lived histories which constitute the relational totality of the personal world. Thus, the relational totality of the "you and I" confirms that the personal world is cultural from the ground up. For me, the notion of the personal world as cultural means that personhood is not an abstract entity. My personality expresses my cultural history. (pp. 24–25).

This is not to imply that mainstream, conventional psychology totally ignores culture. Clearly we find acknowledgment of culture in ethnography and some humanistic approaches, such as person-centered therapy. A critical psychological approach will go further, claiming that culture always exists in dynamic social relations of power (Pinderhughes, 1989). Social power structures such as class, gender, race, and sexual orientation are included in the study of the personal world. According to Sullivan (1990),"The role of critical interpretation is to draw attention to these power relations and bring to light inequities of power. The interest of critical interpretations is *emancipatory*; that is, it challenges the status of social relations where there are gross inequities in power" (p. 25).

A critical interpretation can be said to be *normative* (as opposed to *epistemological)* in that it attempts to bring to awareness systems of power relations under which people suffer. To clarify further, epistemology in psychology appears to place theory over practice. The emphasis is developing a good theory, leaving "the practical life to the philosopher and lay person" (Sullivan, 1990, p. 27). The shift from a strictly epistemological view to a critical normative view is an outcome of Hegal's and Marx' philosophies. The contemporary form of this shift was developed further by Jurgen Habermas.

The conception of the personal metaphor comes out of the notion of "knowledge constitutive interests" (Habermas, 1972, 1974), which are "shapes of what counts as the objects and types of knowledge" (Sullivan, 1990, p. 28). In other words, Habermas tried to *name* categories of intellectual interests in which people ought to focus. He identified three primary cognitive interests: (1) empirical—analytic sciences; (2) historical hermeneutic science (hermeneutics meaning the science of interpretation); and (3) critical emancipatory social science. Sullivan explains the conception of the personal metaphor in relation to these primary cognitive interests: "It is hermeneutical in nature because it systematically takes as its tasks the problem posed by the interpretation of the symbols. The peculiar task of a psychological discipline in this regard would be in the development of some forms of interpretation to deal with individual life histories embedded in cultural forms" (p. 29). The personal metaphor is an attempt to develop an interactive psychology that is founded on the assumptions that individual selves are agents whose actions intend meaning. This is in direct opposition to the American concept of the self—that of being self-contained and individualistic (Sampson, 1977). The personal is always in relation to another, and meaning is found in the expressive relationship between individuals. Remember, too, that in this context, the term *persons in relation* is also expressing culture.

Habermas' (1972) third cognitive interest—the critical emancipatory interest— lays the foundation for the development of a critical psychology and the personal metaphor. The process of interpretation from a critical standpoint is based on certain assumptions (Sullivan, 1990). First, a critical interpretative psychology is self-reflective in nature. In other words, since the interpretation is embedded in history, then the interpreter must acknowledge that he or she is operating from a biased vantage point. Self-reflexivity in interpretation is the acceptance of this bias and the incorporation of the implications of this prejudice. One way to do this is to accept the fact that whatever the interpretation may be, it is bound by the time, space, and history of that moment; therefore, the concept of truth is dynamic rather that static.

Second, the concept of freedom and free acts of individuals and groups is a fundamental concept in a psychology based on critical interpretation. There is a strong assumption of relational freedom in the meaning of the personal world. This very conception embodies an emancipatory interest. According to Sullivan (1990),

This conception of psychology is a part of an emancipatory social science. Its uniqueness in contradistinction to conventional social science is its expressed cognitive interest in *emancipation*. The self-reflection of a critical inquiry brings to light social relationships within society based on power and sustained by inequities of power (regarding domination). The emancipatory cognitive interest brings to light these inequities of power (e. g., between men and women) and attempts to provide a system of self-reflection that will end in a transformation of these relationships of domination. (p. 30) [a reference used by Sullivan from Fowler, 1974]

Such a transformation as Sullivan describes would create a set of relations between persons and groups that is based on a communication that is not grounded on domination and oppression. "A critical interpretative psychology announces social structures which build up a personal world and human projects and denounces, through its interpretations, social structures that destroy the personal as we conceive it" (Sullivan, 1990, p. 30).

The Self as an Agent

From the critical interpretive standpoint, human behavior is understandable only in terms of a dynamic social reference. Because of this, the fundamental unit of analysis must be that which happens between and among people (you and I), rather than an isolated individual. As was mentioned earlier, most personality theories are egocentric. That is, they exclusively focus on the I, not the I–thou. Thus, a critical interpretation expands the framework of traditional psychological analysis.

A critical psychologist contends that individuals use expressions because they intend meaning for others, hence, the self is an agent of communicative acts (De Boer, 1983; Sullivan, 1990). It is contended that human acts are meaningful, complex forms that are interpretable.

The conception of people as agents acting out of meaning is a rather nonconventional notion in psychology. In traditional psychological arenas, people are seen as *patients* who are in need of treatment. Here, we see the person as the agent who initiates or transforms his or her conditions. When people are seen as restricted in their ability to act upon their world, then we limit the scope of our understanding of human behavior (Sullivan, 1990).

Human intentions must be viewed in a relational manner, that being in communication with another or others (De Boer, 1983). The spirit of human intentions is their relational and open-ended element. This is evident whenever intentions must be modified in order to make interpersonal interactions work. When this does not occur, one is called rigid, bullheaded, or stubborn. To explain further:

The person's own self and the selves of others are both then discovered together in relation to one another; they are reciprocally determined within the same categories as one another. In other words, to be me I need you: I need you to respond to my movements for me to appreciate that my movements have consequences in you. I need you to respond to the meaning in my action for me to appreciate that my action does in fact have meaning. (Shotter, 1975, p. 110)

The concept of a relational quality of human action produces a requirement of a personal mode of interpretation.

According to critical psychology, freedom of responsible action depends on four conditions: (1) that there are such things as intentional desires, motivations, and so on; (2) that intentions have behavioral consequences; (3) that intentions are not reducible to variables of the physical environment or to variables of physiological processes (Chein, 1972); and (4) that intentions must be capable of undergoing reflective examination or deliberation (Sullivan, 1990). There are three types of conditions for an action: constitutional, environmental, and motivational (Chein, 1972). These conditions can limit freedom of behavior, as the following explains:

Behavior is free to the extent that the environment and the constitution do not dictate or preclude a particular action, the greater the degree of freedom that exists within the limits of the imposed constraints. Within the limits of these constraints the behavior that actually occurs is determined by the motivation of the actor. No behavior is ever completely free, some degree of freedom being lost as a consequence of the constraints of constitution and environment but degrees of freedom are also gained from the dependabilities of constitution and environment. The gains and losses, however, do not cancel each other out because they are different in kind. In addition, with respect to any particular behavior, some degree of freedom is lost to the constraints imposed by competing behaviors. A person may be free to the maximum degree that the environment and constitution permit it and to the extent that, *(sic)* he does not lose degrees of freedom from constraints imposed by motivational conflicts, sacrifices relatively trivial motives, and effectively sequences or integrates the others. (Chein, 1972, pp. 33–34)

It can be said, then, that there exist structures of freedom, and within these structures of freedom there are tensions among the components. Always, the responsible agent (having personal powers that make a difference in the outcome of action), not only acts but also suffers action which is partly out of their control. Sullivan (1990) calls this "patienthood." This "patient experience" results from external factors, such as the environment, and competing internal motivational factors. Free, responsible acts fall within the dialectic of agency and patienthood. Although lengthy, the following selected passage from Sullivan (1990) succinctly draws together these ideas:

This dialectic is quite complex and subtle, as we know from our own personal experience. To think of ourselves as only agents is pretentious. To think of ourselves as patients is to attempt to excuse all our actions as beyond our personal powers. Responsible freedom is limited freedom worked out within the dialectic of agency—patienthood. The prayer, "God grant me the serenity to accept the things I cannot change, the courage to change the things I can, and the wisdom to know the difference" expresses this complex balance. To talk of "human freedom" and "responsible action," though, in the end assumes that the self as agent incorporates its own patienthood (i.e., self as subject). Individual persons and the wider community proper have the responsibility of creating institutions that enhance the use of personal powers. I call this "human project." At the individual personal level, to relinquish the possibility of using one's personal powers is irresponsible action—you might say, "playing the patient." At the larger level, the creation of societal institutions that rob humans of their personal powers, that is, their capacity for responsible action, is by definition an alienating society. (p. 46)

Critical psychology emphasizes the linguistic quality of human action. It is anticipated that a person's actions are expressions for others, and that these expressions have meaning for others. Sullivan (1990) makes the following contentions: "It is not always easy for agents to find an audience for their expressions, but in the end there must be some audience, however sparse, to make the judgement of the significance of the act. There is no such thing as a significant act in itself. The meaning or significance of a human act is the place that it occupies in a network of *relationships* [Chein, 1972]. Therefore, there is no such thing outside a relational context" (p. 46).

To summarize, human beings are actors whose actions are communicative expressions which, since they are made to be interpretable, are meaningful. The personal mode of interpretation is favored over the mechanical or organic due to the unique characteristic features of the human act: consciousness, intentionality, intention, responsibility, and significant. For each of us, there exists a *personal world* that is comprised of an interrelation of human actions involving communicative acts. The personal world is a relational event and a cultural form (Sullivan, 1990).

The personal world and all of its relationships are inset in a specific history, a real historical event as opposed to an abstract formation of an ideal person. Therefore, the personal world is located in culture. According to Sullivan (1990),

The personal world must be studied dialectically in relation to larger structural totalities. The role of a psychological interpretation of the personal world is simply to accept the microsocial world of the personal without making an individualistic fetish of it as does traditional psychological theorizing. We do not talk about A persons in the abstract. Rather, we talk about black persons who are black Americans, French people who are French Canadians. Persons are persons only within a cultural world. There is no person if there is no cultural form. (p. 73)

Here, the concept of the person is historical, making a critical interpretation of the personal world a journey into biography. A biographic psychology innately calls attention to the life span of the individual as a site of psychological enlightenment (Hudson, 1972). To identify the dialectical factors of the personal world that emphasize the development of human freedom or limit personal freedom is to engage in a critical interpretation, a critical psychology.

FEMINIST THEORY/PSYCHOLOGY

As has been previously argued, traditional psychological theories and practice are not applicable nor appropriate for all individuals and groups. Feminist theory applied to psychology provides several vital theoretical shifts that are needed in order to bring about current-day relevancy to counseling. The following is a brief description of feminist psychology.

In many ways, feminist psychology can be identified as including several key concepts of critical psychology. This meaning that feminist psychology embraces a critical investigation of traditional psychiatric and psychological theory and practice. Identified within this investigation is the premise that there exist three ruling myths. According to Greenspan (1983), "these myths can be stated as follows: first, the myth that the individual's psyche can be understood apart from the specific society in which s/he lives; second, that psychological symptoms can be understood apart from a person's social relationships; and third, that the patient's behavior in therapy can be understood apart from her relationship to her therapist" (p. 16).

A major ambition of early feminist psychologists was to promote the understanding of women's experiences within their societal context and to create nonsexist theories of female development. Feminists have identified four general biases, sexist notions, within therapeutic services. These biases are (1) fostering traditional sex roles; (2) expectations and devaluation of women; (3) sexist use of psychoanalytic concepts; and (4) responding to women as sex objects, including the seduction of female clients (American Psychological Association, 1975). Also noted was the predominance of men in the profession and how these men maintained positions of power over their female clients. "This unquestioned power of men over women paralleled the social order in which men defined women's needs and characteristics, and on this basis passed judgements about women's optimal functioning" (Good, Gilbert, & Scher, 1990, p. 376).

In order to transform this habitus, women began to see themselves as agents with the ability to change their *personal world*. In terms of critical psychology, they lived their *project*, or the significance of intentional human action. There are several major principles of feminist therapy that are applicable to oppressed groups, thus not limiting their application to just women.

The first concept is the recognition that the personal is political. This means that the personal and the political cannot be separated (Gilbert, 1980). Personal problems must be considered within their societal context; for example, the availability of childcare, or the failure of an employer to implement a flex schedule, or job-sharing for working parents must be considered in understanding the makeup of personal stresses and conflicts.

The second concept is the encouragement of women's anger. The traditional role and socialization of women and other oppressed groups is to be cooperative, quiet, and agreeable, especially to men and those with power. It is considered socially inappropriate (an ideological symbol) for a woman to show anger, aggression, or assertiveness. Feminist therapy encourages women to express all of the options open to them, including the expression of previously tabooed emotions. This is considered an emancipatory psychological concept.

The third concept views the therapist–client relationship as egalitarian. When the therapist is seen as an equal partner in the therapeutic process, then the counselor's role as "expert" is de-emphasized. The client then holds the same amount of power as the therapist, which works to eliminate a dominant–subordinate relationship. The therapeutic process becomes one of the client accepting her personal world and her ability to discover options that have the potential to solve her problems, thus transforming her lived experiences.

The fourth concept advocates female therapists for women. As more women seek women therapists, the mutuality of women's issues becomes legitimated in psychological research and practice. The power structure in the profession begins to equalize, making the presence of women acceptable and credible. What went unquestioned in the past is now at the forefront of investigation. An example is the challenge of sexist aspects of psychodynamic theories (Gilbert, 1980). This last concept can be generalized to other underrepresented groups in psychology and psychological services: persons of color, gays and lesbians, the working class, and so on. As members of these subordinate groups are advocated as professional members of psychological services, perhaps their human projects will encourage group liberation.

A CRITICAL PSYCHOLOGICAL FOUNDATION OF COUNSELOR EDUCATION

Critical psychology has the potential to add to the constructs counselors use to make sense of their clients, themselves, and the world. Counseling is now clearly being influenced by today's society, with its emphasis on diversity, skepticism, relativism, and discourse. According to William Doherty (1991), "We are swimming in a sociocultural river whose waters can both nourish and drown us. If we pay attention to the whole river, and not just our small rivulet, we may be able to make choices about our direction, instead of either being swept mindlessly along or stubbornly clinging to the Truth we need to believe in and become fossilized on the river bottom" (p. 42). Counselor educators must heed this warning by rethinking the theoretical frameworks to which we cling. By paying attention to a larger sociocultural reality, we too may be able to make choices about the direction of school counseling. Those antiquated, rigid notions about human nature and behavior need to be loosened and newer, more relevant approaches need to be considered. Our challenge is to learn how to effectively counsel in a world that is not quite the same as the world in which counseling originated (O'Hara & Anderson, 1991).

Yet, it is important to note that we must not leave all traditional notions behind. Perhaps an important skill for counselors is the ability to shift from one theoretical position to another with ease and grace, as the moment demands. To move into the future, counselors need to have one foot in traditional psychological terrain and one foot in a world that has multiple approaches to reality, or better labeled: shifting sands.

Expanding Psychological Constructs

Several critical and progressive psychological constructs have been presented in this book. The following is a synopsis of five constructs that need to be incorporated into current and future counselor education.

First, a more open idea of what the self is and what human beings are is vital in our current and future sociopolitical contexts. According to Maureen O'Hara and Walter Anderson (1991), "We are beginning to see that people can be not only multicultural but multiepistemological--able to find truth and meaning in many ways" (p. 25). The concepts of nonintegrated self-identity, fragmentation, and multiple definitions of self are psychological borders that must be explored. There is a need to expand the dimensionality of identity to include the acceptance of multiple identities. There is a need to define the self-in-relation, thereby including culture, class, gender, sexual orientation, and other aspects that help create the reality of self.

Second, the addition of a third metaphor in psychology, that of the *personal,* provides a language in which to express culture in relation to others. This moves away from the analysis of individuals, to the inclusion of a person's "web of significance," or human cultural expressions. When an individual's culture is added to the picture of who and what they are, the picture expands in all dimensions. In other words, they become social and historical beings. No longer are individuals viewed as only objects, but as objects and subjects at the same time, with relational freedoms. This notion greatly advances multicultural counseling systems of beliefs due to its fluid ideology and the embodiment of culture within personal expression. No longer would future counselors be exposed to cultural issues in bits and pieces (if at all). When counselor educators accept and embrace a personal metaphor as a way of understanding human nature, then multiculturalim would be woven throughout the curriculum.

The third construct is the framing of theoretical assumptions with an overriding inquiry and concern for concealed power relations. Critical questions must be asked about who benefits from the advancement of particular dogmatic theory. Examples of such questions are, "If this theory is truth, to whom or to what does it give power"? and, "From who or from what does it diminish power"? As was discussed earlier, the imbrication of critical theoretical inquiry onto counseling provides a path toward more democratic and just practices. Yet this type of reflection and rational dialogue needs to be skillfully and consistently nurtured in future counselors. Therefore, counselor educators must be able not only to articulate the principles of critical theory, but also to embrace fully the spirit of liberatory purpose.

The fourth construct is the identification of research practice as nonneutral, as opposed to the scientific assumption of value-free. When research studies and results are examined for the value-full position of the researcher, the politicalimplications of the findings are unmasked and exposed. This process works to disempower the dominant cultural influences upon subordinate groups.

The final construct, gleaned from feminist theory, is the identification of biases found in psychological theory and practice. This promotes additional caution against oppressive forces, as well as defines intolerances in counseling practices. Even with the advances made with the gay and women's movements, antisexist laws, and increased public awareness, gender bias, racism, homophobia, and all other "isms" are still prevalent in society. Counselor educators must take a firm stand against all biases and discrimination, both inside and outside of the classroom.

The Changing Role of the Counselor

Professional counselors are viewed as authority figures by society in general (Byrne, 1995). They also have been described as *change agents,* assisting clients in the achievement of desired psychological, social, and career goals. The role of the counselor historically has been defined by traditional psychological theory and practice. When a paradigm shift occurs in any theoretical arena the role of the professional who practices the theory must also shift. Therefore, the following is a preliminary discussion of a shift in the role of school counselors and counselor educators for the twenty-first century. This discussion follows the pedagological shift as purported in this dissertation.

In conjunction with the premises set forth in this book, and in light of the growing complexity in our society, the following three identifiable elements of change in the role of the counselor emerge.

First, borrowing from feminist theory, counselors need to see their work as political. Feminist theory has identified ways in which traditional psychological theory politically perpetuates biases against women and devalues women's perspectives. By advancing feminist theory beyond women, one can identify additional ways in which traditional psychology perpetuates biases against those living in the margin and devalues their perspectives. Feminists contend that the personal is political and therefore counseling, which deals with the personal, is political in nature as well. According to feminist theory, "[A] basic principle [is] that the personal is political and reflects a proactive stance designed to eliminate oppression in women's lives and empower women" (Enns, 1993, p. 50). This means that the client's concern or problem cannot and should not be removed from its societal context. An example in school counseling would be the availability of a parent to attend a counselor conference, a child's inability to concentrate in class, or the cutting of funds for a self-esteem guidance program.

All of these instances have political implications: The parent cannot leave work for fear of loosing income or a job; the child may not have adequate food in his/her home due to a shortage of food stamps, and therefore concentration is difficult; and finally, the school board cut funds in order to support a more publicly endorsed program.

Another component that makes counseling political is the position and practice of the counselor. If the counselor quietly supports the status quo, then she or he may well be perpetuating oppressive politics. This is done, most often unknowingly, because the counselor has not been exposed to the critical theoretical position as affirmed here. Although, as counselor education programs begin to take a stronger social and political stand against oppression and toward more liberatory action, future counselors will have the wearwithall and skills to make substantial contributions to democratic schools. In this context, the label "change agent" takes on a new dimension, that of revolutionary.

The second element, again taken from feminist theory, is the shifting role of the counselor, from a position of power and authority to one of *coexplorer* through the complexities that comprise the client's life. This has several important consequences for both the counselor and the client. For the counselor this may mean crossing psychological theoretical borders involving the denorming of dominant cultural values, beliefs, and behaviors and the respecting of relational realities. The depth, scope, and fluidity of the counselor's world view is a critical factor in the ability to facilitate this shift in frame of reference.

Feminist psychology speaks to the establishment of an equalitarian relationship between the counselor and the client. This creates a power-sharing effort in the therapeutic process. No longer is the counselor seen as the almighty way-shower, the one with all of the answers. No longer is the client seen as a helpless, sick, or inferior. Equality in counseling relationships comes out of the creation of mutual dialogues of respect.

The third element of change deals with counselors becoming critical leaders. It is important to note that even though equalitarian relationships are established, it does not mean that the counselor will not take a leadership position when necessary. Power-sharing does not mean that the power is *always* equal; rather, effective counseling, as suggested in this work, involves *power-shifting* between the counselor and the client throughout the counseling process. At times, the counselor must be a leader through the psychological and emotional confusions that exist in a world of constant uncertainty. Just as critical educators, counselors must see clients as having the innate ability to identify contradictions in their lives and act as agents to bring about social and personal changes. Although counselors need to work in collaboration with their client and other relevant persons, including parents, teachers, administrators, social workers, and others, there will be times when the counselor must take the lead in advancing progressive practice. This may include unmasking injustices in schools and communities, confronting hegemonic forces, remapping norms that have oppressive powers, and moving others past either–or thinking. Preparing counselors to take on these roles must be part of their educational experience. They must be able to maintain a delicate balance between leadership power and openness to the acceptance of difference.

Greater client empowerment is a major result of the shifting role of the counselor. The client and, in the case of schools, the student begin to see themselves as *the experts* in their own lives, as opposed to seeing the counselor as the expert. The goal of counseling "is to enable clients to find new meanings in their life situations and to 'restory' their problems in ways that free them fromthe mesmerizing power of the dominant culture" (Doherty, 1991, p. 38). As the client is able to come to terms with his/her ability to break away from socially constructed definitions of mental health, identity, success, and so on, he/she begins to develop self-appreciation and self-understanding.

As a way to review the salient elements and major contributions of this chapter, the following points are offered:

1. Aspects of critical psychology work to uncover further contradictions between the beliefs, customs, and values of the ascendant culture and the lives of oppressed groups.

2. In order to promote liberatory action, psychology must be partisan, that is, for the individual human agent, not the dominant culture.

3. Expanding the metaphors used in psychology allows for the inclusion of culture, gender, life-style, class, race, and other contributors to the self.

4. For each person there exists a *personal world*, which is comprised of an interrelation of human actions involving communicative acts. The personal world is a relational event and a cultural form.

5. From feminist theory, we begin to acknowledge the linkage between the political and counseling, equalitarianism, and advocacy.

6. The roles of the counselors must shift in order for them to truly be "change agents."

There is one remaining aspect regarding the changing paradigm of counselor education, and that is the influence of our time in history. Because it is hoped that the theoretical foundation presented here will better prepare counselors into the next century, it is paramount that we examine a philosophical movement called *postmodernism*.

6

Counselor Education in Postmodern Times: Taking Critical Theory into the Future

Left to be swallowed by the darkness that exists outside the concreteness of historical and collective struggle, desire transforms itself
into fantasy, endlessly in pursuit of what it lacks. Yet critical reason
can give desire wings, so that thought can be lifted beyond the
limitations of the present moment in order to be transformed into
dreams of possibility. And with dreams we can do wonderful things.

—Peter McLaren
"Schooling the Postmodern Body"
Journal of Education

Most traditional psychological theories and practices grew out of a philosophical
and historical time, coined *modernism,* when it was believed that scientific
principles could be applied to just about any topic for the purpose of greater
understanding (Jones & Wilson, 1987). Modernism peaked during the 1950s and
1960s when the need for singular understandings of reality gave comfort to a
world that was seeing changes through newly developed technologies. Those
who supported this philosophical approach have been called *structuralists,
positivists, functionalists,* and/or *modernists*, depending upon to which camp
they belonged. Nonetheless, their belief was that there exist universal notions of
truth through scientific answers. The old religious and naturalistic truths became
passe, and purity, reason, and order became the standard. The creation of
psychiatry and scientific management of humans were hallmarks of modernism's
desire for measurement above belief (Tierney, 1993).

FOUNDATIONS OF MODERNIST EDUCATION

The philosophical foundation of modernism is found in scripts written by
white men whose works are held up as models of high culture and civilization. It

was assumed that these writings could be applied universally because they were believed to be scientific truths. Such writings later will be labeled as "grand narratives." Of major importance to this project are the ways in which modernism influenced education and psychology.

American education as we know it stems from the basic notions of modernality. Educational theory and practice supports a faith in the modernists ideals that highlight an individual's capacities to think critically, to exercise social responsibility, and to change the world in the name of freedom and justice. Educational structures also function to encourage the undisputed belief in, and legitimization of, the greatness of the modernists' ideals. According to Stanley Aronowitz and Henry Giroux (1991),

education provides the socializing processes and legitimating codes by which the grand narrative of progress and human development can be passed on to future generations.

The moral, political, and social technologies that structure and drive the imperatives of public schooling are drawn from the modernist view of the *individual* student and educator as the guarantor of the delicate balance between private and public life, as well as the safeguard who can guarantee that the economy and the democratic state will function in a mutually determining manner. Within the discourse of modernism, knowledge draws its boundaries almost exclusively from the European model of culture and civilization. (p. 58)

To question the canons of modernism is to question the very definitions and meanings of schooling. "In effect, to challenge modernism is to redraw and remap the very nature of our social, political, and cultural geography" (Aronowitz & Giroux, 1991, p. 58). Yet, in view of the changing societal horizon, perhaps what once served as an educational and psychological cornerstone needs to be reshaped. It is time to deterritorialize modernism and remap its political, social, and cultural boundaries to include racial, gender, ethnic, and life-style differences.

MODERNIST PSYCHOLOGY

As with education, modernism had a great influence on the development of psychological theory. One of the most prominent characteristics of modernist psychology is that the individual is stripped of the cultural and social contexts that comprise his or her lived experience. William Tierney (in McLaughlin & Tierney, 1993) offers some clarity in the modernist interpretation of identity and self:

A modernist assumes that a life history can accurately describe an individual's identity based on common criteria of what counts as objective knowledge. Faith in reason allows the modernist to believe that empirical investigations create singular, accurate versions of a "true" self. Many modernists would argue that the advent of psychology helped us understand the motivations of the human psyche and self. From this perspective we interpret [a person's] life story as a singular narrative measured against other individuals' life stories. A unitary version of identity and self are employed. Gergen comments, "Problems such as phobias, homosexuality, depression, and the like [are] equivalent to malfunctions" (Gergen 1991a, p. 42). From a unitary understanding of self, [one's] life would be judged against norms such as how well he [she] adapted or assimilated in terms of race, class, and sexual orientation. This view, assumes that law-like generalizations of the world and the self exist and that our investigations enable us to determine how one might better be able to conform to common standards. (pp. 126–127)

As you may recall from the previous discussion of traditional psychology, the researcher or scientist sees himself as an unbiased, neutral interpreter of the "truth," much in the same way as schools identify their status as neutral conduits of knowledge. The researcher, therefore, has the power to define and describe the ideal identity, self, and community. Here, a person's history is used for the sole purpose of illuminating "universals such as truth; the relationship between the researcher and the researched is relatively unimportant as long as the researcher subscribes to generally accepted rules about how to study objective reality" (Tierney, in McLaughlin & Tierney, 1993, p. 127).

FROM MODERNISM TO POSTMODERNISM

As a challenge to modernism, the 1970s and 1980s brought about the beginnings of what is called *postmodernism.* Some postmodernists saw modernity as indentifying with individuality, enlightenment, science and technology, the industrial and political revolutions, and, thus, democracy and freedom. Still other, more radical postmodernists interpret modernism as repressive, homogeneous, and domineering in terms of epistemology, sexuality, politics, and culture (Kellner, 1988).

Postmodernism can be defined in multiple perspectives and viewed through multiple lenses, for example, theoretical and philosophical, psychological, societal, and personal. The following is a brief look through these lenses, and, just like looking through a kaleidoscope, at times the images overlap and blend together.

The term postmodernism comes from the structural transformations and conditions experienced in an era of late capitalism. These include: "an increasingly radical change in the relations of production, the nature of the nation-state, the development of new technologies that have redefined the fields of telecommunications and information processing, and the forces at work in the growing globalization and interdependence of economic, political, and cultural spheres" (Aronowitz & Giroux, 1991, p. 62). To further elaborate, post-modernism is

inextricably related to the changing conditions of knowledge and technology that are producing forms of social practices of modernity. For Lyotard [1984], the postmodern is defined through the diffusion throughout Western societies of computers, scientific knowledge, advanced technology, and electronic texts, each of which accents and privileges diversity, locality, specificity, and the contingent against the totalitizing narratives of the previous age. . . . Technical, scientific, and artistic innovations are creating a world where individuals must make their own way without the benefit of fixed referents or traditional philosophical moorings. Total mastery and liberation are dismissed as the discourses of terror and coerced consensus. In its place postmodernism appears as an ideological and political marker for referencing a world without stability, a world where knowledge is constantly changing and where meaning can no longer be anchored in a teleological view of history. (Aronowitz & Giroux, 1991, p. 60)

Postmodernists claim that capitalism has lost its once cohesive structure. This has influenced the following elements that help to make up the postmodern condition: (1) the deconcentration of capital as national corporations lessen regulation of national markets; (2) changes in the labor force due to deindustrialization, which created a shift in the centers of production and a decrease in the need for blue-collar workers; (3) a rapid increase in white-collar workers as well as a new service class; (4) the emerging of new cultural/ethnic/political formations along with increased cultural diversity; (5) financially collapsing inner cities forcing demographic shifts, which result in the growth of rural and suburban populations; and (6) "the appearance of an ideological/cultural apparatus in which the production of information and symbols not only becomes the central aspect of the making and remaking of everyday life, but contributes to the breakdown of the division between reality and image" (Lash & Urry, 1987, in Aronowitz & Giroux, 1991, p. 65).

A Deconstruction of Notions of Truth

A major philosophical and theoretical premise of postmodernism is the rejection of universal "truths," also called *grand narratives*, and totalizing thought. Because of this, postmodernists force a movement aimed at redefinitions of previously unquestioned universal concepts. Their contention is that there can be no single ideas of the common good since some groups and individuals within society always will be silenced because of their differences from the norm (Tierney, 1993).

Postmodernism rejects the belief that experts control interpretation. A consequence of this is that the relationship between researcher researched shifts from one of powerful–powerless, where one holds the knowledge and the other is kept in the dark, to a relationship where each is a collaborator and a participant. Thus, relationships equalize and a power shift occurs. When experts no longer have the control over interpretation, the notion of singular truths vanishes. The ground is then fertile for multiple interpretations, which lead to conflict and competing interpretations. In fact, conflict is desired because it means that different interpretations of reality are being voiced and discussed. "The post-modernist struggle, then, is to generate oppositional realities and deconstruct singular interpretations of truth" (Tierney, 1993, p. 128). Unlike other movements and politics that claim the possibility of total democracy and social justice, postmodernism acknowledges that such is impossible, that there will always be antagonistic elements. To further explain,

It [postmodernism] views all forms of agreement as partial and provisional and as products of given hegemony. Its objective is the creation of a chain of equivalence among the democratic demands found in a variety of movements—women, blacks, workers, gays and lesbians, or environmentalists—around a radical democratic interpretation of the political principles of the liberal democratic regime. Such an interpretation emphasizes the numerous social relations where subordination exists and must be challenged if the principles of equality and liberty are to apply. (Mouffe, 1990, p. 63)

According to Henry Giroux (1988a), "Postmodernism not only makes visible the ways in which domination is being refigured and redrawn, it also points to the shifting configurations of power, knowledge, space, and time that characterize a world that is at once more global and more differentiated" (p. 162). Knowledge in postmodern times is always seen as partial, historical, and social in nature. Therefore, postmodernism "offers a series of referents for rethinking how we are constituted as subjects within a rapidly changing set of political, social, and cultural conditions" (Giroux, 1988a, p. 164).

Postmodern Psychology

In terms of psychology, the postmodernist rejects the notion that self and identity are defined in terms of universal concepts. In other words, postmodern psychology decentralizes modernists' scientific labels in order to reconfigure systems of power and to create a psychology that is relevant to the times in which we live. Through an expanded postmodern interpretation, the old individualistic world view is replaced with a "relational reality" (Gergen, 1991a). Here, multiple-fluid identities allow for the acceptance of difference, diversity, and mutual dialogues of respect (Tierney, 1993). Yet, this is in clear contrast to the traditional teachings of the congruent individualistic self—the True Self that is the same in all contexts.

The postmodern framework of a fluid nature of identity and self mirrors the cultural conditions of postmodern times. It is a time when one must create a survival strategy in a world of constant uncertainty (O'Hara & Anderson, 1991). It is a time when one can select from among a myriad of realities, life-styles, values, attitudes, opinions, and personalities at any given time. According to psychologist Kenneth Gergen (1991b), "As every new choice invites a sea of mixed opinions and speculations, both from outside and from the multiple voices we have already collected within ourselves, the possibility of national choice fades away. When one can see the situation in multiple ways, how is one to discern the 'best' or the 'right' way?" (p. 28). Social change has brought about shifts in how we see ourselves and others. Self-identities have become fragmented and, again according to Gergen (1991b),

Are not all the fragments of identity the residues of relationships, and aren't we undergoing continuous transformation as we move from one relationship to another? Indeed, in postmodern times, the reality of the single individual, possessing his/her own values, emotions, reasoning capacities, intentions, and the like, becomes implausible. The individual as the center of cultural concern is slowly being replaced by a consciousness of connection. We find our existence not separately from our relationships, but within them. (p. 28)

This concept is strongly realized through glimpses of postmodern culture and experience. A few examples are the shifting configurations of family structures, the labeling of extended relationships as "family members," the deep attachments formed between child and daycare provider, relationships established and maintained solely through electronic means, and even bonds created with stars of favorite television programs. The fourth force in counseling, multiculturalism, is expanded with postmodern's deeper meanings of culture and experience.

CRITICAL POSTMODERNISM

The fusing of what appear to be opposite theoretical ideologies, critical theory and postmodern theory, is called *critical postmodernism*. Critical theory grew in scope and application during modernist times when scientific rationality and reason were believed to be the path to truth. In contrast, postmodernism challenges the modernists' notions of rationality, norms, and identity. Through the exploration of the fundamental characteristics and philosophical tenets of these two theories, one discovers a foothold in which to secure a counselor education paradigm shift. To this end, I will describe the concept of critical postmodernism and how its application to counselor education can best serve our purpose of preparing school counselors for the twenty-first century.

Critical Postmodern Theory/Pedagogy

Postmodernism represents a theoretical stance that forces a rewriting of modernisms' scientific rationality "as to effect a shift in power from the privileged and the powerful to those groups struggling to gain a measure of control over their lives in what is increasingly becoming a world marked by a logic of disintegration" (Aronowitz & Giroux, 1991, p. 115). This shift began in the late 1980s when the ways in which progress and history are defined and measured loosened up and new multiple references began to take hold. As you may recall, for the postmodernist alternative forms of knowing began to hold credit, and universal notions, such as identity, were rejected.

New ways to engage knowledge have been suggested by postmodernists Stanley Aronowitz and Henry Giroux (1991). The concept of *border crossing* and *border pedagogy* provides a perspective from which one can conceptualize students and teachers recognizing the limitations and boundaries of dominant discourse and *moving across* such borders in order to engage a more complete relevancy of the knowledge. Border pedagogy allows for multiple realities such as different cultural codes, languages, life-styles, experiences, and frames of reference. When one engages knowledge as a border crosser, one moves in and out of boundaries created around points of difference and power. It is important to note that, in order to be engaged in border pedagogy, one must be resistant to the authority maintained by modernists' notions of universal truths and grand narratives that are based on white, patriarchal, and class-specific versions of the world. In other words, one must be critical of traditional knowledge and cross over into new realms of meaning. Just as frontier explorers bravely traveled and crossed foreign lands, clearing a trail as they went, so too must border crossers blaze new trails while they negotiate and rewrite maps of knowledge, social relationships, and values. According to Aronowitz and Giroux (1991), "Border pedagogy decenters as it remaps. The terrain of learning becomes inextricably linked to the shifting parameters of place, identity, history, and power" (p. 119).

A key concept of border pedagogy is the awareness that there exists some body of valid information that has been placed outside the sphere of legitimate wisdom. In other words, there is knowledge other than that which has been validated and perpetuated by grand narratives. It is said that this knowledge, along with its holders, have been silenced and kept in the *margins*. The postmodernist believes that "knowledge forms emanating from the margins can be used to redefine the complex, multiple, heterogeneous realities that constitute those relations of difference making up the experiences of students who often find it impossible to define their identities through the cultural and political codes of a single, unitary culture" (Aronowitz & Giroux, 1991, p. 120). Opening the dimensions of knowledge to include marginalized constructs frees previous restrictions as to what is defined as knowledge of value. Pop cultural elements and informal means of acquiring social knowledge work to expand a formally stringent scientific base. This is a direct challenge to modernisms' reliance on totalizing ideologies that were founded on the premise of safety in absolutes.

The concept of border crossing is an example of a powerful and progressive movement of combining the most insightful elements of the modernist and postmodernists philosophies. As stated by Aronowitz and Giroux (1991),

We believe that by combining the best insights of modernism and postmodernism, educators can deepen and extend what is generally referred to as critical pedagogy. We need to combine the modernists emphasis on the capacity of individuals to use critical reason in addressing public life with a critical postmodernist concern with how we might experience agency in a world constituted in differences unsupported by transcendent phenomena or metaphysical guarantees. (p. 117)

So, what are the best insights of modernism and postmodernism, and how might these insights be fused? William Tierney (1993) provides a guide map through this sometimes confusing and foreign territory. In comparing the basis of critical theory and postmodern theory, Tierney (1993) explains, "Critical theory is an attempt to understand the oppressive aspects of society in order to generate societal and individual transformation [Fay, 1987]. Postmodernism challenges the cultural politics of modernist notions of rationality, norms, and identity" (p. 4). As was described earlier, critical theorists want to identify the oppressive nature of society, and once this is understood by those oppressed, these individuals and groups will then change their world in order to liberate themselves. Due to the major focus on inequality and sociopolitical forces, critical theory supports the notion that all knowledge is socially and historically determined and is a consequence of power (Tierney, 1993).

In contradiction, postmodernism questions the ability to achieve social justice and democratic life through the process of rationality or through reason alone. "Thus, rather than struggle to enable groups to overthrow anything, postmodernism attempts to develop multivocality and to understand difference" (Tierney, 1993, p. 5). For the postmodernist, the complexity of difference becomes a central organizing concept. Because total agreement is not the aim, nor the expectation, differences in voice and multiple representations are acknowledged. In a time when the multiplicity of images, realities, and social identities are formed through the mass media, there must be room for valid differences. Our images are composites of complex social and cultural forces.

Because critical theory in general fails to deal with differences, it is most beneficial to incorporate a postmodern view. Here, the idea of difference does not reject the ideal of understanding across differences. Dissimilarities are seen as borders that are recognized and crossed; culture is a borderland that is in constant transition (Anzaldua, 1987). Postmodern theory rejects notions of what constitutes norms. Therefore, unlike modernist concepts of difference—that which "places those of us who are different constantly in relation to what is conceived as 'normal' and something to be desired" (Tierney, 1993, p. 7)— postmodernists place difference in terms of power and knowledge. Post-modernism works to decenter power, which diffuses margins; "And in doing so has made room for those groups generally defined as the excluded others" (Giroux, 1988a, p. 166).

It is important to note here that postmodernists do not want to create another "melting pot" consciousness by doing away with the diversity in our society. Rather, they wish to unmask the pervasive power of the norm. They contend that there is great strength in diversity. This stance is well positioned by Tierney (1993): "Understanding difference affords individuals the possibility not only of understanding other people's lives, but also of coming to terms with how they are situated within society, how their specific identities are framed and shaped by society" (p. 10). As notions of critical theory and postmodern theory are blended, an advocacy for empowerment, the development of voice for oppressed people, and denormed notions of difference emerge. Again, norms are decentered and difference becomes the organizing concept. One result is an open dialogue with previously "silenced" people.

The postmodernist rejects categories because they disallow the fluid nature of postmodern times. A prime example relevant to this discussion is the category of identity. "Knowledge and identity are always partial and constructed, forever subject to multiple interpretations and reconfiguration" (Tierney, 1993, p. 10). The notion of *relational reality* is advanced by postmodernists. That is, in a world of shifting, multiple realities, it seems most appropriate to embrace these insights about the fluid nature of categories. When this is combined with critical theory's goal of revolutionary change, the table is set for the development of "mutual dialogues of respect" (Tierney, 1993, p. 17).

Some recent work among postmodernists dovetails nicely into concepts being advanced by progressive counselor educators. William Tierney (1993) poses a crucial question: "How do we create understandings across differences so that we are able to acknowledge and honor one another, rather than bring into question one another's legitimacy?" (p. 27). Developing forms of understanding is the cornerstone of counseling. Yet in these challenging and changing times, counselors all too often fail to understand themselves, let alone their clients. The critical postmodern theoretical approach may well help advance efficacy in school counseling.

Critical postmodernism (Giroux, 1992) frames the questions and discourse in a way that provides an unmasking of oppressive unequal relationships of power and, at the same time, creates hope in the notion of crossing over, not out, differences. According to Tierney (1993), "Critical postmodernists see the individual as both object and subject in history, and locate action within a sociohistorical realm that gets acted out on a cultural terrain that is contested, redefined, and resisted. People are neither passive objects incapable of resistance, nor are they unconstrained individuals able to determine their own histories" (p. 28). And finally, Tierney (1993) offers, "Critical postmodernists break boundaries and struggle to enter border zones with the realization that to do otherwise simply maintains traditional positions of power and authority. And the idea of identity is broken down with the recognition of the multiple and often conflicting identities we simultaneously hold as we span borders" (p. 29).

The horizon of Western culture is changing. The human skyline is shifting— from that of uniformity—to that of diversity; from unquestioned support of class dominance to struggles for liberatory human action; from quiet acceptance of determinism to naming the world of the oppressed and finding a personal voice. In order to be legitimate, psychological interpretation, notions of identity, decentering of norms, border crossings, and practice must align with this shift.

No longer does traditional, conventional education and counseling address the human conditions of the masses, if, indeed, it ever did.

CRITICAL POSTMODERNISM AND COUNSELING

Even after this abridged look at postmodernism, one cannot ignore the stark changes that have taken place in the last 20 years and how these changes have had a tremendous impact on day-to-day lived experiences of individuals and groups. Unfortunately, counselor education theory and practice have failed to keep up with the global changes that have occurred, let alone those changes that will continue to happen as we prepare for the twenty-first century.

Counselor educators have the ethical, intellectual, and professional responsibility to provide students and clients with the most accurate and current information and experiences, as is understood in the ethical codes and principles of counselors and psychologists. It is not only an ethical responsibility to offer relevant, progressive, and future-oriented instruction, it is a moral and humanitarian duty as well. Counselor educators are in the position to take constructive political action through teaching, modeling, and professional activities that encourage human understanding and equality.

The utilization of critical postmodern theory to rethink and retool counselor education provides a new perspective on defining difference, interpreting truths in psychology and counseling, and ultimately clearing the intellectual, historical, and emotional spaces for positive change.

Shifts in Personal World Views and Personal Constructs

People resist change, even if the end result is positive (Schlossberg, 1989). Change is difficult because there is always an element of the unknown, and unknowns are usually uncomfortable. We tend to cling to that which is known, even if it is not working for us, rather than risk something that is new and different (Bridges, 1980). In order to bring about the intellectual and emotional shifts needed for an expanded theoretical foundation of counselor education, *internal* shifts first must occur within the hearts and minds of educators and their counseling students. To help explain this required step, I have selected a theoretical position of the psychologist and scholar, George Kelly (1955).

Our way of making sense of things depends on the ways in which we make meaning in the world (Ivey, Ivey, & Simek-Morgan, 1993). Personality theorist George Kelly (1955) contends that people interpret or construe events according to their own unique view of the event. This unique way of looking at and interpreting the world is called a *personal construct*. These personal constructs are developed over the course of our lives. Our repertoire of constructs increases as new experiences, people, and events evolve. Kelly believes that these personal constructs need to be refined, altered, expanded, or even extinguished as new life experiences are encountered. There is nothing absolute or final about any construct; therefore, they are fluid in nature and open to change. Even though a postmodernist may interpret this theory as a "universalist grand narrative," it has merit in this context due to its nonuniform nature and tolerance of difference.

The composite of personal constructs formulate what is called an individual's *life* or *world view* (Byrne, 1995). A counselor's life view is comprised of a multitude of constructs, among which are how they believe humans should think, feel, and act if they possess good or "normal" mental health and appropriate values. Most often, counselors are not aware of their own life views because they have never fully questioned or examined the impact, bias, or oppressive consequences their views may have upon others. In a society of diverse and multiple cultures, realities, sexual preferences, class structures, and experiences, conflicts in life views are inevitable. Richard Hill Byrne (1995) provides the following examples of some possible conflicting life view assumptions and values that counselors and clients may hold:

- Humans are completely free to act by rational choice when faced with decisions; or behavior is determined only slightly by reasoning, and more by internal and external stimuli not accessible to reasoning.

- Morals are natural, apparent to everyone, and equally inborn to everyone (or required by a supreme being); or morals are learned, culturally determined social codes.

- Humans are a higher order of animal life; or human existence has a transcendent or spiritual aspect that differentiates it from animal life. (p. 20)

In a multifaceted world, there are hundreds of possible conflicts between the life view held by the counselor and the life view embraced by the client. Therefore, counselor educators must not only create ample opportunities for future counselors to become aware of their own life views and the values and assumptions embedded in those life views, but they also must help students critically question the power their life view may have in a clinical setting. Of course, before this can occur, the counselor educators themselves must have this awareness.

A critical postmodern theoretical foundation provides the framework for challenging oppressive personal constructs and life views. Through the pedagogical process described in this book, students are able to unmask those forces within society, education, psychology and *themselves* which have contributed to silencing individuals and groups. Hence, the work of counselor educators becomes political, with the project being social symmetry.

Defining Difference

The infusion of the postmodern denorming notions of difference with critical theory's advocacy for empowerment and the development of voice provides a dynamic template for personal, cultural, and societal understanding. Post-modernists call attention to the harmful and oppressive ramifications of norms.

A prime example of the negative results of norming is the way in which counselors are trained to use and interpret an assortment of educational, personality, and career assessments. In each of such assessments, counselors compare their client's results against that which has been deemed "normal." Up until recently, most assessment tests were normed by using predominantly white middle-class populations. Thus, the validity of test results of any other population other than white middle-class students was questionable, at best (Facundo, Nuttall, & Walton, 1994). Although norming groups are becoming more diverse in an attempt to mirror society and some counselor education programs are incorporating more multicultural issues, adequate inclusion of multiple voices and realities has not been realized. Students are still categorized, grouped, and educated according to statistical norms and test results. Counselors must be educated to critically question the power of norms and work to diffuse such power when it results in the marginalization of others.

Future counselors must be able to sift through modernism's discourse in order to negotiate and rewrite maps of knowledge, social relationships, and values. As was discussed earlier, this means crossing borders—moving outside of the scientific, absolute definitions of truth. Therefore, counselor educators must incorporate and validate nontraditional material, beliefs, and world views in their classrooms and field activities. This means shifting from seeing difference in relation to that which is conceived of as normal and desired to viewing difference as an accepted reality. Clearly, we are talking about an inclusionary mission, putting effort into assuring that there is an end to marginalizing practice. Counselor educators are in leadership positions—able to influence a movement toward accepting differences and working from those differences to build solidarity (Tierney, 1993). In order to accomplish this, we must hear and honor multiple voices and relational realities.

Shifting Notions of Truth in Counseling

Interpreting the concept of "truth" as multifaceted, fluid, and relational is a central notion leading to the ability to denorm and then honor differences. With this as a foundation for analysis, counselors would critically question the relevancy of theory and practice in the individual context in which it is applied. In other words, counselors must be skilled at decomposing supposed truths in order to test their appropriateness in a world that is in constant motion and change. An example is the belief (truth) that an emotionally healthy individual possesses a congruent identity at all times. This belief dictates that behavior is consistent with a personality "type" and therefore can be predicated. And, going a step further, a counselor can guide this "healthy" individual into the perfect career, one that is in accord with his or her congruent personality/identity.

From a critical postmodern point of view, the supposed truth/grand narrative that all healthy people maintain a constant identity is examined through a perspective that acknowledges the existence of multiple and competing realities. What might it mean to cross this border and enter the notion that individuals are healthy if they have multiple identities for multiple realities? It means that I function from one identity when I am among my significant culture group and another identity when I function on the job, and yet another identity when I am with my intimate partner. This concept rejects the notion that experts control interpretation and further discounts the idea that a singular version of truth can exist (Mclaughlin & Tierney, 1993).

The concept of multiple identities and relational realities is disconcerting to modernists who have worked hard to create absolutes in human behavior. After all, if fluid identities exist, then how can they be predicted and controlled? Understanding behavior is always complex, but this notion adds enormously unpredictable variables that are difficult to categorize and measure. From a postmodernist perspective, multiple identities and relational realities fit nicely into the goal of revolutionary change and the development of mutual dialogues of respect. It may well be through this process that counselors expand their once narrow world views to tolerance and respect of difference.

THEORETICAL CONSTRUCTS OF COUNSELOR EDUCATION FOR THE TWENTY-FIRST CENTURY

As a way to get to this point, we have journeyed through many theoretical perspectives: multicultural counseling, critical theory, critical psychology, feminist theory, critical pedagogy, postmodernism, and critical postmodernism. Each of these perspectives has offered new elements and constructs that give credence to the pedagological shift needed in counselor education. This has been a journey of questioning, gathering, evaluating, and applying selected notions that support equality and justice.

There exists a *centrality of inclusion* in this expanded theoretical foundation of counselor education. Although the implications for this pedagogical shift have been alluded to throughout this book, a summary of the major themes is as follows:

1. The acknowledgment that the current theory and practice of counselor education is inadequate in light of multiculturalism, postmodernism, and efforts to promote equality and social justice.

2. The critical questioning of relations of power in society, psychology, education,

and the role of the counselor, and the consequential outcome of oppression.

3. The acknowledgment that all persons are historical and social beings with the ability to act as agents in their own lives.

4. The creation and allowance of "power shifts" in the counselor–client relationship.

5. The embrace of a reality that is (1) relational and multidimensional in nature, and (2) transforms a once rigid position of an absolute notion of truth to more fluid, multiple, and inclusionary notions of truth, such as multiple identities.

6. The decentering of norms that work to diffuse the power inherent in that which is deemed "normal."

7. The seeing of counseling as political in nature and practice.

8. Assisting future counselors in developing the skill, ability, and courage to critically think, evaluate, question, and act for the purpose of liberatory outcomes and the crossing over of difference.

The ultimate goal of this work is the reconceptualization of knowledge itself, of education, of counseling, and of social structures. From this position, it is clear to see that the traditional theoretical platform was not only incomplete, but that it was also incorrect. The errors of an exclusionary position perpetuated a well-established imbalance of power. Feminist postmodernism offers a most poignant and appropriate observation: "no one standpoint is adequate, but that reality is embedded in complex relationships, historical contexts, and social constructions. Instead of pursuing one truth, inquirers must recognize that knowledge is not neutral and focus on how meaning is negotiated or discovered, and how people in power control meaning" (Enns, 1993, p. 25). This book does not contend that the position taken here is the only reality, nor that the theoretical foundation proposed is adequate. Rather, we must each take the time, effort, courage, and spirit necessary to negotiate and discover our own truths.

REFLECTIONS

As a counselor educator, I recently visited a middle school to evaluate a counseling graduate student enrolled in a multicultural fieldwork course. The visitation included the observation of the counselor conducting a small student group counseling session. The topic of discussion was how they all, in one way or another, were struggling with feelings of frustration. One student spoke of how no one listens to her. Several students lamented over poor treatment from some of the teachers, "They don't care about how we feel or what we think." One young girl shared how she had to be responsible at home for her bothers and sisters, but at school she couldn't seem to be very responsible. Another student shared her confusion about what she should choose among too many options. And one student feared she would be hurt by gang members on campus.

The counselor trainee conducted the session as she had been taught: paraphrase content; reflect feelings; be warm and empathetic; and facilitate behavioral change in order to help the students succeed in school. The only acceptable version of reality here was attending class, doing homework, not getting into trouble, and autonomously being responsible.

I heard cries for help that the student counselor had not been trained to hear. I heard the voice of resistance. I heard the voices of those suffering from oppression. I heard voices of lives that were fragmented, saturated, and alienated. Afterwards, I wanted to somehow "replay" the session and assist the students in a dialectical exploration of their experiences. I wanted to help these student cross new borders of understanding, not only about the times and conditions in which they live, but about their ability to make meaning for themselves. I am not sure what the outcome would have been, but I believe the risk would have been worth taking.

While it is impossible to replay that counseling session, it is not impossible to adjust the theoretical framework that informs counselor preparation. While much of what is taught is appropriate and valuable, it is not enough. The inclusion of critical theory, pedagogy, psychology, and postmodernism in counselor education curriculum embraces elements of hope for schools which, as described by John Dewey (1966), would provide the basis for a society built on equality and reciprocity among people.

"By challenging the commonsense assumptions that are inscribed in the dominant ideology of discourse and power, it becomes possible for [counselor educators] to reconstruct their own theoretical frameworks by adding new categories of analysis and by rethinking what the actual purpose of their teaching might be" (Aronowitz & Giroux, 1991, p. 93). Of course it will take courageous, progressive, and even radical counselor educators to bring about such changes. The road ahead is full of struggle, and, as with any border crossing, guards protecting the status quo will try to stop our progress.

Progress means creating environments where different voices are heard and everyone is a learner; where tolerable discomfort in the classroom is encouraged, so long as it is combined with mutual dialogues of respect; where climates of tolerance promote the seeking out of diverse viewpoints; and where we strive to understand one another's pain and views of the world. As counselor educators we have the ethical and moral responsibility to prepare counselors for the next century who personify humanism, democracy, and hope at its best. With solidarity in vision and the honoring of our own diversities, we can accomplish this mission. It is hoped that this work will provide a partial roadmap for the journey.

7

Teaching Counselor Education for the Twenty-First Century: An Application to an Introductory Course in Counseling

This book has set forth several theoretical tenets involved in a pedagogical shift in counselor education. It is important to note that, even though the theoretical ideology has been presented, there has been no attempt to impose a "prescription" as how to teach such ideology. Yet, for the purpose of articulation, the last two chapters of this book describe applications of critical postmodern counselor education to classroom settings at a midsized California State University campus. This chapter discusses instructional and curricular application to an introductory educational counseling course. These discussions include some background information about the selected university, a description of the program and its requirements, examples of how critical postmodern theory can be incorporated into the context of the classroom, teaching tools created and utilized, and samples of student comments.

The last chapter of the book provides an application of critical postmodern counselor education to a more advanced educational counseling course, multicultural counseling at the same university.

CALIFORNIA STATE UNIVERSITY, SAN BERNARDINO

The San Bernardino campus of the California State University system is one of 20 such campuses. Serving inland Southern California, in one of the fastest growing regions in the nation, the university's goal is to "prepare students to assume leadership roles in the twenty-first century" (California State University, San Bernardino, 1994, p. 11). The university opened in 1965, offering six degree programs to approximately 300 students. Today, the curricula has expanded to 42 baccalaureate degree programs, 15 teaching credential fields, and various options within 19 masters' degree programs. Current enrollment exceeds 12,500 students.

California State University, San Bernardino, serves residents living in the largest county in the United States. It is not unlikely for students to drive over

100 miles to attend class. Also, this region of the state is extremely diverse in terms of race, ethnicity, and culture; the student population represents similar diversity.

THE EDUCATIONAL COUNSELING PROGRAM

As part of the School of Education, Department of Advanced Studies, the Educational Counseling Program provides professional preparation for the Pupil Personnel Services credential with specialization in School Counseling (Masters of Science, 72 quarter units). It also provides preparation for Masters-level counselors in other educationally related settings (Masters of Arts in Education, Counseling option, 48 quarter units). The program is designed not only to support the definition of educational counseling as delineated in the California Education Code, 49600, but also to expand this definition with the inclusion of an overall design that is consistent with stated rationale based on recent theory and scholarship. Therefore, the framework for the Educational Counseling Program is defined in the following organizing theme: "The Counselor as Collaborator with multidisciplinary, multicultural helping systems to foster life skills development of students in educationally related settings" (Reilly, 1994, p. 4). The above organizing theme is defined further:

Collaboration: Working together, sharing efforts on behalf of pupils or their representatives for the purpose of promoting life skills development. Connections are circular rather than hierarchal, and there is no "less than" or "greater than" in terms of power or influence.

Multidiscipline: Recognizing counseling and guidance's ties to education as both a science and an art, then to social sciences, primarily psychology (counseling, vocational, educational, developmental, social, and clinical), then to sociology, political science, and the physical and natural sciences (medicine, biology, chemistry), law, humanities (art, literature), and theology.

Multicultural: Recognizing counseling's sensitivities to the diversity of racial, ethnic, cultural, gender, age, and life-style orientations of students and their families.

Helping systems: The organizing delivery models used by various groups to assist persons in addressing their difficulties in life skills acquisition or fulfill to the greatest degree possible their potential for such acquisition.

Life skills: Those personal, social, psychological, and physical competencies, attitudes, and behaviors which permit persons to achieve their maximum potential as healthy individuals and members of society.

Development: A normal and continual process of biological, intellectual, moral, and psychological growth (Reilly, 1994, pp. 4–5).

The theme is supported by the professional commitments of the faculty articulated as the epistemological beliefs and ethics agreed upon as essential to the program. These are (1) counselors are educators as well as professional counselors; (2) each student is valued, has worth, and can succeed; (3) each student functions as a system, with physiological and psychological components, and that affects, behaviors, and cognitions organize this operation; and (4) each student also functions within a system, with bonds and affiliations that develop over the course of the student's life. These may be bonds with one person or others who are similar in terms of other variables, for example, ethnicity, culture, gender, nationality, age, and so on (Reilly, 1994).

Program Design

The program design includes a philosophy and purposes; assessment statements of desired results for candidates; and an associated rationale for coursework, field experiences, and program evaluation. The program's primary philosophical base is the application of science to education and psychology, as in Dewey's (1966) version of pragmatism, or instrumentalism, which sees ideas and thoughts as instruments of action to reshape human environments. Pragmatism's basic tenets of optimism, emphasis on action, and belief in the future undergird the notion of the counselor as scientist–practitioner. The importance of experience-based learning is also part of this philosophy.

The program philosophy and purpose enhances and compliments the philosophy and purpose of the Pupil Personnel Services, school counseling specialization, as defined by the California Teacher's Credentialing Commission (California State Department of Education, 1991):

To prepare pupils to become literate and responsible citizens. . . . to promote personal growth and to develop critical thinking skills so that pupils become caring family members and motivated workers. . . . to recognize that in addition to intellectual challenges, pupils encounter personal, social, economic, and institutional challenges. . . . strategies are essential to address these challenges, promote success, and prevent educational failure. . . . to be pupil advocates and to provide prevention and intervention strategies that remove barriers to learn. . . . in partnership with educators, parents, and the community, to maintain high expectations for all pupils, facilitate pupils reaching their highest potential, foster optimum teaching and learning conditions, and prevent school failure. . . . because California's pupils live in a dynamic society with a diversity of cultures and changing values, they have needs for educational environments that prepare them to function in complex, global, and multicultural communities. . . . the needs of pupils demand that pupil personnel services specialists and others work together by uniting their skills as a team to provide comprehensive, coordinated programs and services on behalf of all pupils and their families.

The program design reflects multicultural and global perspectives that permeate all courses. The extent to which all courses in the program reflect these perspectives is evidenced in the course syllabi, instructional activities, professional development activities for students and faculty, and program evaluation and documents.

The program design has a cogent rationale and knowledge bases from established and contemporary research, the wisdom of practice, and emerging education policies and practices. The pedagogical knowledge base of the program incorporates multicultural and global perspectives, and is operationally defined as "the entire repertoire of skills, information, attitudes, etc., that counselors need to carry out their counseling responsibilities" (Reilly, 1994, p. 6).

Program Curriculum

The curriculum requirements for attainment of the Masters of Science Degree in Counseling and Guidance (including the PPS Credential) are as follows:

PREREQUISITES:

ECLG 531	Introduction to Counseling
EDUC 495	Advanced Writing

DEGREE REQUIREMENTS (72 UNITS):

ECLG 601	Research Methods in Counseling
ECLG 619	Appraisal Procedures in Counseling
ECLG 650	Applied Career Counseling
ECLG 651	Professional School Counselor
ECLG 654	Legal and Ethical Issues in Counseling
ECLG 632	Advanced Psychological Foundations of Education
ECLG 633	Advanced Study in Child and Adolescent Development
ECLG 655	Multicultural Counseling
ECLG 656	Counseling Theories and Techniques
ECLG 657A	Counseling Practicum
ECLG 657B	Counseling Practicum (school based)
ECLG 658	Consulting with Parents and Staff
ECLG 678	Theory and Practice of Group Counseling
ECLG 679A	Counseling Fieldwork: Multicultural Setting
ECLG 998	Advanced Seminar in Educational Counseling
ECLG 999	Written Counseling Comprehensive Examination

Eight units (2 courses) from:

ECLG 679B	Counseling Fieldwork: Elementary School
ECLG 679C	Counseling Fieldwork: Middle School
ECLG 679C	Counseling Fieldwork: High School

Four units (1 course) from:

ECLG 659	Secondary School Career Counseling
ECLG 696	Special Topics in Counselor Education
ESPE 635	Effective Communication with Professionals and Families
ETEC 623	Technology in School Administration and Counseling

The Faculty

The faculty consists of seven full-time faculty and a number of part-time instructors who serve as the needs arise. One faculty member serves as the coordinator of the program. The full-time faculty is comprised of four women, one African American, one Native American Indian, and two white; and three men, all white.

The Students

The program serves approximately 150 students. A survey of the student population was conducted in the fall of 1994 ($n = 47$). The results of this survey showed that 17 percent were males and 83 percent were female; the mean age was 34.2 years. Ethnicity data indicated a fairly diverse student population: 19 percent African American, 5 percent American Indian, 2 percent Asian, 14 percent Latino, 57 percent white, and 2 percent other. The majority of the students had jobs: 22 percent reported working over 40 hours per week, 56 percent reported working between 21 and 40 hours per week, and 14 percent worked less than 20 hours per week. The average number of hours spent studying outside of class per week was 12.74 (Reilly, 1994).

THE "TWENTY-FIRST CENTURY PROJECT": AN APPLICATION OF CRITICAL POSTMODERN THEORETICAL FOUNDATIONS

This section discusses how a critical postmodern counselor education framework functions within the enterprise of a classroom, specifically, in an introductory course in counseling. Since one of the tenets of this theoretical position is infusion into the total curricula, the class chosen for this project was a small (six students) ECLG 531, Introduction to Counseling, class conducted in the fall quarter of 1994. This is a prerequisite course to admission into the program and one that challenges the students' personal views about themselves, others, and life.

ECLG 531 Class Requirements

An experienced-based instructional approach in counseling and its techniques is utilized for this course. The course provides students with opportunities to explore the field of counseling and the professional career options related to it. The course is also designed to permit the student and the instructor to evaluate the student's potential as a counseling professional. In this sense, the course is used as a "screening" tool, to screen program applicants as to their readiness and appropriateness of counseling as a career choice. Therefore, this course is taken prior to application to the program. In fact, students complete the application process as part of the class requirements. This process differs from other traditional graduate-school application process whereby the student must be accepted prior to beginning coursework. The process suggested here allows for a more complete assessment of the student's motivation; maturity; ability to learn, demonstrate and critique beginning counseling skills; academic ability; level of self-awareness; and interpersonal skills.

There are several course requirements:

1. Attend and participate in all class sessions. Come prepared for discussions.
2. Complete weekly course assignments including readings, study guides, and additional projects as assigned.
3. Observe and interview one counselor in an educational setting with oral sharing of the interview. (This is to allow the students an opportunity to explore the career.)
4. Write an autobiography that discusses the major people, places, and events of their life and how those people, places, and events have influenced the student to want to become a counselor.
5. Complete a midterm exam and a final exam.
6. Prepare two videotapes, according to specified guidelines that include extensive self-critique, which demonstrate the student's ability to engage basic beginning counseling skills with a partner. These tapes are viewed and critiqued by the instructor in class.

In addition to the above, students are also asked to volunteer to be a client for an advanced student in the program. This involves a four-to-five-session commitment.

The "Twenty-First Century Project"

Students were informed in the first class session that they would be participating in a trial set of lessons for the purpose of exploring instructional units that were under consideration for the program. They were also informed that the topics covered were part of the instructor's special research project that hopefully would be published in the future, and that their full participation was greatly appreciated. They were briefly told that they would receive a workbook that would guide them through four short instructional lessons. The students were informed that the workbooks would be collected on the last night of class and kept by the instructor; however, if they wished to have their workbook back, they could pick them up in the next quarter.

By way of introduction, the instructor discussed themes within the lessons and the range of potential emotional responses the students may experience as a result of exploring uncomfortable topics, such as unmasking oppressive forces in society, the unearned privilege that some people have, and the unveiling of bias and prejudice. The honoring of all student "voices" was a main effort of all classroom activities. To accomplish this, the following guidelines were established:

1. Maintain confidentiality at all times. Confidentiality is one of the most important ethical principles, the hallmark, if you will, that governs the establishment of trusting counseling relationships. One is more likely to share intimate, personal, and sensitive information if there is trust and a commitment to keeping the information between, or among, those disclosing. In a classroom setting, a guideline of confidentiality encourages the forming of a trusting, working bond among the students and the instructor. This is especially valuable in an introductory counseling course, as the students are asked to practice a component of the ethical code in which they must ascribe to as a professional counselor.

2. Actively participate in all of the activities, discussions, and exercises to the very best of your ability. Many beginning counseling students are unfamiliar with the experiential approach to learning. They are accustomed to the "banking" method of teaching, whereby the teacher "deposits" knowledge into the empty minds of the students (Freire, 1970). The student in this sense is seen as a passive learner. This second guideline sets forth the instructor's expectations of the student. Learning is seen as an exchange among all of those in the classroom. Often, students are uncomfortable with this level of engagement and intimacy. Those who like the traditional straightforward lecture–exam format, must quickly decide if this approach is for them. Since the counseling process mirrors engagement and intimacy, these beginning counseling students can use this classroom environment to gauge their readiness for counseling training against their level of comfort with this teaching approach.

3. Exercise positive regard and respect for others and their contribution to the class. This guideline allows for the early introduction of Carl Rogers' (1951) elements in establishing trusting relationships. These elements are nonpossessive warmth, unconditional positive regard, and empathy. Students are asked to stretch their tolerance of opinions and experiences that are different from their own. The acceptance of others and what they bring to the learning process is mandatory to begin mutual dialogues of respect.

4. Maintain an open mind and a willingness to consider views, values, beliefs, and life-styles that are different from your own. New ideas and shifts in life views can only begin with open minds. As classroom discussions become uncomfortable,

tense, or even heated, it is most helpful to remind each other of this important guideline. Since all students, and the instructor, agree to adhere to this guideline at the beginning of the course, it works to maintain growth toward greater understanding.

5. Work to acknowledge your own resistance and be willing to explore its meaning. This may mean challenging your beliefs about yourself, others, and life. The existence and theory of resistance (see Chapter 3) is discussed with the introduction of this guideline. The instructor used self-disclosure of personal experience with her original resistance when engaging with some of the same controversial theoretical concepts. This had tremendous impact on creating an environment whereby resistance can be identified, explored, and processed. One indicator of resistance is language and attitude that involves the following: "all or nothing," "black or white," right or wrong."

6. Exercise the courage needed to explore new ideas, to explore your feelings and reactions, and to be honest. It is acknowledged that this type of intentional interaction, self-exploration, and the questioning of well-established ideology takes courage. As an introductory course in counseling, this is an appropriate time to discuss also the courage it takes to take any risk in life, especially entering therapy or counseling. This creates an excellent bridge that connects theory with practice. This discussion and guideline works to set up the expectation of risk taking by the students and the instructor.

The instructor carefully reviewed the introductory portion of the workbook, including the rationale behind the above guidelines, with the students during the second week of class. The four units of instruction and activity were conducted on the third, fifth, seventh, and ninth weeks of class, this out of an 11-week quarter.

The Students

From the demographic information requested in the workbooks, the following data were obtained. The participants were comprised of five women and one man with the age range from 26 to 48 years. The mean age was 37.5, with a median age of 38.5; thus, this particular group of students was slightly older than the mean age (34.2 years) of the students in the 1994 survey. The ethnicity of the class proved to be very diverse, with one Latina, one East Asian/Egyptian, one Russian/Jew, one African American, and two white. The students were asked their religious affiliations, and the responses were two Christian, one Catholic, one Jewish, one Religious Science, and one left the question blank. A question of marital status showed that one-half of the students, three, were single, one divorced, one married, and one separated.

All of the students had aspirations of entering the counseling profession. One student had a Marriage, Family, and Child Counselor license and wanted to complete the requirements for a Pupil Personnel Services (PPS) credential. The rest were just beginning the program. One student, a male African American, displayed inappropriate behavior the first and second weeks of the class. When challenged about this, he selected to drop the class; therefore, he did not participate in the workbook activities.

The Life View Questionnaire

Since a premise of this theoretical shift is the process and outcome of shifting personal life views, an instructor-developed Life View Questionnaire was administered the first night of class and then again during the last full class session (excluding finals week). The purpose of this questionnaire was to obtain a broad indication as to the degree (if any) to which the students' life views were altered as a result of this instruction. Additionally, the questionnaire was intended to assist the students in understanding their own life views by posing certain life issues and asking them to respond according to the degree in which they agree or disagree. A four-point Likert scale was used, the response categories being: strongly agree, moderately agree, moderately disagree, and strongly disagree. This was not intended to be a quantitative research tool, but rather a medium with which to increase the students' self-awareness about their own life views.

The students were informed that the exercise does not intend to explore all of the facets of their life view; rather, it is intended to initiate self-awareness and evaluation of potential aspects that make up their personal constructs. The questionnaire contained 15 items. Each item was posed as a statement, and each dealt with a potentially controversial issue. For example, "Women have the right of abortion"; "Counselors should be 'color blind' and treat all clients the same"; "Homeless people are often lazy"; "Gay/lesbian relationships are a natural life-style"; "White people enjoy unearned privileges because of the color of their skin"; "American schools promote social justice and equality"; and "If you live in the United States, you should speak English."

A secondary function of this instructional tool is to "put out there" some constructs of a dominant cultural ideology. Students are able to get a feel for the degree to which they themselves have unquestionably embraced these ideals. By completing the questionnaire again at the conclusion of the course, the students are able to measure, loosely as it may be, life view shifts that might have occurred during the course. During the final class meeting, the students discussed life view changes as part of their personal growth sharing.

The "Twenty-First Century Project" Workbook

The material contained in the workbook is divided into four units. Each of the four units follows the format of the class presentation and outlines key concepts, ideas, and words. The pages are designed so that the student can jot down notes and thoughts that will help him/her complete the exercises/questions at the end of the unit. Each unit has questions that are designed to assist in the processing of the theoretical ideas presented. Additionally, these questions provide a means to explore further the students' lived experiences with the concepts. For example, the students were repeatedly asked to relate a topic to an event, relationship, or emotion that they had experienced and write about it. And lastly, each unit offers a "Journal Entry" page for the students to write their thoughts and feelings about the material and experience.

The topics for each of the units were selected for their appropriateness to the themes of counseling in the twenty-first century as identified and explored in this book. The following is a discussion of each of the units and the topics covered in each:

UNIT I: INTRODUCTION & PERSONAL CONSTRUCTS—As an introduction, the purpose of the workbook is described as a way to provide a systematic method in which to engage in and reflect upon the concepts, theories, and activities that implement an expanded theoretical approach to preparing school counselors. Also part of the introductory material are the classroom guidelines, which the students are asked to honor.

Just following the introductory page is a very brief demographic information survey. This includes name, telephone numbers, gender, current occupational/ employment, marital status, number of children, ethnicity, age, undergraduate degree major, and counseling career goal.

This unit covers the concepts of developmental perspectives regarding shifts in personal ideas and attitudes; personal construct theory (Kelly, 1955) and the possible origins of our own life views; what the term "lived experience" means, in other words, we all do not experience life in the same ways, and some ways are not legitimated by segments and institutions within our society; and lastly, the concept of difference, biculturalism, oppression, and white privilege are introduced.

The unit concludes with five self-exploration questions. As with all of the units, the students are given about 10 minutes to answer the questions. They then are asked to form small groups, three to four students in a group, and discuss their answers to the questions or any other issues raised as a result of the unit. The questions for this unit are "After completing the Life View Questionnaire, how would you describe your life view?" "What were the origins of your original views on the topics included in the questionnaire?" "How do aspects of your life views change over the years? What were the causes of those changes?" "Identify how your life views are different from others in your discussion group."

UNIT II: EXPANDING THEORETICAL CONCEPTS: CRITICAL & FEMINIST THEORY—This is a rather lengthy and dense unit which could very well be separated into three units. The unit as is contains two sections. The first section covers the very basic concepts, history, and characteristics of critical theory. This includes class-consciousness, hegemony, a dominant culture, oppression, ideology, the relationship between power and knowledge, universal principles, dialectics, and the application of critical theory to pedagogy.

The second section deals with the salient issues of feminist theory. Those selected

for this instructional activity are traditional psychological myths, the creation of nonsexist theories, the concept that "personal is political," equalitarian relationships, and the feminist theme of developing a "voice."

If this unit were divided into three separate, shorter instructional activities, they should be (1) Critical Theory; (2) Critical Pedagogy; and (3) Feminist Theory.

Due to the volume of material introduced in this unit, the students are asked to consider the following seven questions at the end: "How and why do critical theoretical concepts differ from the concepts that you have been taught and believe? " In what ways does critical theory 'feel right' to you? How and why?" "Considering what you now know about critical theory, can you identify any contradictions in your lived experience, past or present? Describe." "In which relationships in your life have you had power? How and why? How did it feel?" "In which relationships in your life have you experienced oppression? How and why? How did it feel?" "How might a feminist theoretical approach increase effectiveness in counseling persons of color, gays and lesbians, those of the working class, and/or gang youth?" and "Does this new awareness (theory and exploration) affect your old life view? If so, how and why?"

UNIT III: AN AGE OF DIVERSITY: THINKING ABOUT PSYCHOLOGY—This unit contains two sections, and, as in the previous unit, this could be divided into two separate class sessions and activities. The first section challenges traditional thinking about psychology in an age of diversity. The topics covered are major aspects of traditional psychology, including the two metaphors of mechanical and organic; Western ideology and psychology; application of critical theory to psychology, including the shift from value-free science to value-full approaches; and seeing the self-as-agent.

The second section of this unit introduces the basic concepts of postmodernism. During this presentation it is most vital for the instructor to engage free-flowing dialogue among members of the class, for example, brainstorming the influence of everyday culture that deals with the multiplicity and complexity of living in a technological age. Through such discussions additional salient aspects of postmodernism can be identified, such as the importance of everyday culture; the nature of legitimate knowledge; the importance of relevance of theory to practice; the need for interrogation and exposure of absolutes and meganarratives; establishing faith in social transformation ("Difference becomes central, norms are decentered, and dialogue remains a possibility" [Tierney, 1993]); and lastly, the postmodern notions and role of difference, multiplicity, fluidity, pluralism, and the nature of "truth."

There are seven questions for self-exploration in Unit III. They include: "What are your thoughts/opinions/feelings about 'blaming the victim?'" "Respond to the concept that *no behavior is completely free*" "Identify ways in which your life contains issues of multiplicity" "In what ways has your cultural knowledge been validated as legitimate?" "In what ways has your cultural knowledge been denied legitimacy?" "To what degree do you believe society can be transformed? How?" "How can school counselors impact social transformation?" and, "Does this new awareness (theory and exploration) affect your old life view? If so, how and why?"

Due to the previous critical thinking, discussions, and concepts introduced, the groundwork has been laid for open engagement of ideas pertaining to biases and exclusions found in traditional psychology. It is important to note that these students are working with a traditional introduction to counseling textbook during this course. The contradictions between traditional theory and critical theory/ psychology that are discovered during this lesson provide a rich and fertile arena for discussion and personal growth.

At this juncture the emphasis of the self-exploration questions and small group discussions begin to evolve toward counseling, personal responsibility, and the potential of counselors to impact social transformation. This gradual transition seems to be a natural movement toward the last unit of this project.

UNIT IV: A THEORY OF CRITICAL POSTMODERNISM & COUNSELING—This final unit covers the salient premises of counseling challenges of the future, as articulated in this project. The key points covered by the instructor are (1) the vital need for expanding personal life views; (2) the function of questioning contradictions in everyday lived experiences; (3) personal constructs of cultural systems; (4) the concept of adaptive identities as articulated in postmodern psychological literature; (5) equalitarian relationships; (6) an expanded role of counselors, in other words, political stance for equality and social justice; and, (7) following up on the expanded role of counselors, the notion that all counseling is political.

Discussion topics include the requirement of counselors to maintain open and flexible life views; the need to question the biases, exclusions, and contradictions found within counseling theory and practice; to cross *over* differences, not *out* differences; to establish equalitarian relationships and help the client to know that he/she is the expert in his/her life, not the counselor; to see the role of counseling and of the counselor as political in nature; and the need for maintaining a fluid interpretation of realities.

The self-exploration questions for this last unit are "Do you see yourself as being more tolerant and accepting of diversity as a result of this project? Describe and explain." "Has your concept of counseling changed as a result of this project? How and why?" "Review your 'journey' through this project and discuss any emotional experiences that you might have had. What does this mean for you?" and, "To what extent have you shared with others (family, friends, co-workers, partners) information, experience, and emotion connected to this project? Discuss."

Upon completion of this final unit, the students retake the Life View Questionnaire (LVQ). The last journal entry assignment asks the student to discuss how and why what he/she has learned and experienced from the project has affected his/her old world view. Here, students identify and discuss any changes in their responses on the LVQ. The students are encouraged to offer any comments that they may wish to share. Because this occurs at the end of the course, the students generally appreciate the opportunity to express their overall impressions, concerns, and gratitude.

Classroom Climate

The classroom climate was one of openness, acceptance, and freedom of expression. This was due, in part, to the classroom guidelines set forth at the beginning of the project and a required Confidentiality Statement that each student was required to sign as part of the program. This statement explains the ethical standard of confidentiality, and the student agrees to maintain this standard at all times. Another reason for the positive climate was the small size of this course, which is unusual for this university. The students were able to become friends and get to know each other with ease. Although this does occur in other classroom settings, these students formed relationships faster due to the small number of class members. Perhaps the main reason for the open classroom environment was the energy, courage, and genuineness modeled by the instructor. The instructor encouraged conflicting ideas and beliefs. There was time and room for all differences. In fact, she often encouraged students to share their thoughts, feelings, and experiences in order to disclose the reality of difference. What was modeled was the postmodern notion of border crossing and the honoring of relational realities.

Project Evaluation: Student Voice

The opening concept of this project was that of personal constructs and the development of individual life views. The students actively participated in the classroom and small group discussions. They were all eager to explore the origin and components comprising their life views. In responding to the written request asking the student to describe his/her life view today, the students who responded ($n = 5$) all claimed to have a fairly open and accepting mind. Yet, there was evidence of struggles with difference and the impact of culture, as is exampled in the following responses:

> *A 48-year-old African American woman:* I think I have a fairly open mind, though I may still harbor reservations about some life-styles.
>
> *A 29-year-old Latina woman:* I'm pretty open-minded. I think I'm open-minded because of my own life experiences. Coming from another country and trying to integrate two cultures has helped me appreciate the cultures of others.
>
> *A 35-year-old East Indian/Egyptian woman:* I am fairly open and accepting of various life-styles and beliefs. I can accept and respect the fact that an individual's life views may be different from my personal life views, but that does not mean that I adopt their views.

The students explored the aspects of their life views that had changed over the years and what had caused those changes. It was important for the students to recognize that lifes view can change, and, in fact, their own life views have changed during their lives. All but one student responded to this question, and the results indicated that the experience of a personal crisis and/or simply growth and learning created a shift in life view. Through the questions, the students told parts of their own life stories. As was expressed by one student, "My life view began changing dramatically with my divorce from my ex-husband as I questioned how could one stay married forever if marriage was so difficult. I also had to modify some of my views as my older daughter entered adolescence and began embracing values different from my own. I also saw injustice in the workplace and in society which further altered my views." Another female student wrote,

When I first got married, I believed my role as wife was to be taken care of by my husband, while I was to hold honor and respect for my family, bear and take care of our children, and somehow plan to take care of my elders in the future. My views changed when my husband didn't live up to my learned expectations. Changes resulted from realizing that I was not being "taken care of," but was being used. Also seeing my own father, use and take for granted my mother's care toward him.

Upon completion of the second lecture, which pertained to critical theory, pedagogy, and feminist theory, four of the six students responded to the questions in the workbook. Several themes emerged: additional discovery as to the sources of their own previously unquestioned beliefs; a strong agreement and support of critical ideologies; identifications of contradictions within their own lives; and a beginning understanding to the benefits of connecting these theories with efficacy in counseling practice. The following student voices illustrate these themes.

Previously unquestioned beliefs:

The concepts I that have been taught tended to be idealistic and based upon religious principles, i.e., "you are your brother's keeper," "with God, all things are possible," "believe and you shall be saved," "all men are equal."

We are taught to believe what the majority wants us to—we are to repeat without question [the lesson]. Most of the tests [in school] are recall or restate through essay what has been said. Seldom are you asked to question, think, disagree, or explain why you agree with what you've learned.

Agreement and support of critical ideologies:

I like it because it proposes the idea that we should think for ourselves and come to our own conclusions. By doing this we are less likely to follow blindly. We would be open-minded to differing thoughts and beliefs instead of expecting everyone to conform, or be ignored.

It was a pleasure to actually question the norm. I have known for years about how different cultures try to say that there is only one truth.

The ideal of equality among people is still only an ideal and in my thinking is still probably unattainable, given human nature.

It [critical theory] makes sense to me because everyone is influenced by the popular ideologies, cultures, and mood of their own period.

I'd really like to study these concepts more. I would like to understand them better and be able to talk about them with more knowledge base.

Identifying contradictions:

Having been raised in the "Father Knows Best," "Donna Reed" era, I am a walking contradiction. Dominant cultural tradition is my family. Father didn't know best. Mother had to work outside of the home most of the time. My parents were alcoholics. Supposedly, I should be totally dysfunctional but, while I am not perfect, I turned out okay.

Although women have had the right to vote for well over 50 years now, they are far from equal with men, but they are catching up. Women are still viewed and treated as the primary care-givers; they are viewed as domesticated and are in many cases expected to submit to their husbands, even when they have jobs outside of the home.

And, the benefit of connecting theories to efficacy in counseling:

A feminist theoretical approach should increase effectiveness in counseling persons of color, gays, lesbians, the working class, and gang youth—as women traditionally have been a disenfranchised group, subject to great abuse over the centuries and still are in many societies. The same political activities that kept women in subordinate roles have been used to keep other groups down as well.

A feminist approach looks at the person and takes the person into account. Therefore, it would look at the person's whole experience including what it is like being from a different culture.

By helping *all* clients find their own voice, this approach opens up the counselor to help many "groups."

Some responses indicated a struggle with the notion of "blaming the victim." A few of the students clung, at least in part, to the dominant belief that individuals have total choice as to their circumstance in life, as the following writing expresses: "The victim has to accept a certain percentage of the blame except in cases where there's a "loaded gun" pointed at his head. However, the victim usually had no alternatives therefore, they should not be blamed i.e., 'your money or your life.'" Yet another student was quite firm in her belief: "I think its scapegoating. This allows us not to have to look at our own role."

There was pessimistic hope for societal transformation. The students hoped for more equality: yet if it was to be, it would be very slow in coming. Several students identified the need for a greater understanding of differences, that this would be the necessary element for transforming society. Some comments were,

Any transformation in society leading to greater acceptance of people with obvious differences will be slow and long in coming. I believe society can be transformed by education and familiarity with any perceived differences among people.

I am pessimistic about a great change, but I think this society will learn to live with the various differences in people. Certain people will continue to look down their noses at others, but we are here and not going anywhere. . . . I know people who'll be working with kids in education who are fed up with multiculturalism (truly)!!

One student expressed frustration with the uninterested behavior of a fellow classmate: "It's hard to say because it [society] won't be transformed until each individual is willing to open their minds to a new reality. I guess I have hope since in our class, out of six of us, there was only one person who preferred to file her nails than to discuss these issues."

Upon the completion of the last unit and retaking the Life View Questionnaire, the students were asked several questions pertaining to how they perceived any changes in their life views and their overall reaction to the project. They were encouraged to express any feelings they had experienced as a result of these activities. The overall reaction of the students, although the degree of enthusiasm varied, was positive and supportive to this pedagogy. The connection between the value of these theoretical principles to future counseling was substantial. The students saw themselves as more aware and open to differences, as is evidenced by comments such as,

This project helped me to expand my horizons and accept that even as a tolerant person I have my limits and biases. (I'm unlikely to be successful counseling Rush Limbaugh.)

It has opened up windows I believed were there but couldn't yet see.

My main feeling is that I want to study this subject more. I have an instinctive agreement with what I've learned so far. I never knew any vocabulary to express my thoughts. I guess I'm a postmodernist but didn't know it.

I think my concept of counseling has been enhanced by this project. That the normal concerns of people are not only affected by family systems, developmental issues, but also by society and the environment in which one must survive.

It angers me when I find people who would rather not accept multiculturalism as relevant to our society, but who would prefer to remain color-blind. Perhaps this is comfortable to them, but how can one live in this society and not acknowledge diversity?

My old view has been changed somewhat because I have received new information on theoretical concepts, basic concepts, and looking at what's always been accepted as the norm. I find I question things more and realize that there's more than one way to think about something or accomplish it.

As has been discussed, the function of a critical postmodern educational counselor is to be a leader, model, and facilitator of border crossings. Our job is to create an environment whereby students are able to begin to question and critique life. In the project just described, it was important for the instructor to be genuine, self-disclosive, honest, and comfortable with the students' discomfort. There is a wonderful saying in counseling, that one way to bring about healing is to make the unbearable bearable. This is a delicate line that must be walked by counselor educators. That is to say, there must be enough tension in the classroom to allow for intellectual and emotional movement and, at the same time, an element of validation that creates a "bearable" space. This was accomplished in this project, as is evident by the following student comments:

At first, I was skeptical because I didn't understand why you [the instructor] were interested in this subject matter. It's very seldom that someone who doesn't seem to experience these issues is actually interested. Once I got to know you, I understood some of the reasons why you would be interested, then, I became very interested. I would have been happy to have had this subject be the focus of all of our class meetings. I became angry and hurt when I heard someone comment negatively about us doing these lessons. Her indifference also upset me. I was happy to see those who were interested talk and share this subject matter.

I really enjoyed this project. Sometimes the new information was given a little too quickly for me to pick up everything, but it was all so interesting. You've validated me, as a bicultural person, and you've opened my eyes to other life diversities. Thank you!

8

A Critical Postmodern Approach to a Multicultural Counseling Course

The Twenty-First Century Project is an example of overt inclusion of critical postmodern theory and pedagogy as applied to an introductory course in educational counseling. At the same California State University, a similar philosophical and theoretical position was taken in a multicultural counseling course during the spring quarter in 1994. Yet, in this instance, a covert approach was taken by the instructor. In other words, a much more subtle, more latent style of teaching the same themes was utilized. Similar topics were broached gently during lecture, discussions, and group activities. There were no formal "workbooks" or lessons. The following is a discussion of this course and some of the students' comments as to their changed perspectives as a result of the experience.

COURSE DESCRIPTION

The main focus of this course is the diversity of cultural, ethnic, socio-economic, gender, and life-style experiences; the nature of prejudice; and their impact upon the counselor–client relationship. Consideration is given to examining techniques found to be most effective in cross-cultural counseling. The course is designed to increase effectiveness in counseling bicultural and minority group clients. Emphasis is given to client needs based on the uniqueness of racial, ethnic, socioeconomic, and other backgrounds. The common experience of oppression is explored. There is a prime consideration given to a critical examination of contemporary problems. It is important to note that this was the first time that this critical postmodern instructor taught this course. Prior to this change in focus, the course was limited to an exploration of different cultural foods, poems, and customs, as related to counseling. There was no mention of a critical agenda.

COURSE REQUIREMENTS

The course requirements complement the goal of the learning experience: that of becoming aware of culture, biases, and prejudices; that of becoming a border crosser, across differences through increased knowledge; and that of building skills of an effective and caring cross-cultural counselor. The following is a brief description of the course requirements:

- Complete 20 hours of fieldwork experience in a multicultural setting. The purpose of this requirement is to provide the student an opportunity to obtain supervised counseling experience with a diverse population. Students are encouraged to select a site that has a student population which differs from their own cultural background. Students must maintain a Fieldwork Hours Log Sheet and have their experience verified by an on-site supervisor.

- Complete a self-exploration project and share the findings in a small group during class. This involves a written paper that extensively explores the student's ethnic, cultural, and life-style background; feelings of being different; early memories of racial ideology; feelings associated with being a member of their ethnic or cultural group; and experiences they have had in power relationships. The purpose of this assignment is to allow the students to explore and examine their backgrounds, and identify prejudices and biases. This exercise separates ethnicity from race in the examination of feelings, attitudes, and behaviors. For many white students, their first response is that they do not have an ethnicity or culture. This assignment may be the most powerful and meaningful for these students since they must do some "investigation" in order to discuss their heritage. For a complete example of such an assignment, see *Understanding Race, Ethnicity, and Power* by E. Pinderhughes (1989).

- Prepare and present, with a group of classmates, a professional presentation that informs the class about a particular group of people within our society. They are to be multiperspective, multimedia, and multidynamic presentations. Students should not simply stand in front of the class and read their prepared material. There is great emphasis on professionalism, enthusiasm, and personal commitment to the topic. Students are encouraged to present an interesting workshop format that is creative and informative. Each presentation is to be accompanied by a resource and information packet.

    Students are to sign up for one of the following presentation cultural groups: African American, Asian American, Native American Indians, Latino/as, Gays and Lesbians, Disabled, Jews, and Muslims. The presentations, or workshops, are to include: (a) historical perspectives; (b) key cultural concepts, such as values, roles, customs, beliefs, rituals, practices, and support structures; (c) data concerning social/economic circumstances and education; (d) mass media portrayal; (e) art forms and literature; (f) issues in counseling; and (g) approaches and techniques for counseling.

    Ultimately, due to the outstanding breadth, depth, and quality of the presentations, some of these presenters were mentored by the instructor and encouraged to submit presentation proposals to professional counseling conferences.

- Complete a midterm examination that is based on assigned readings, class discussions, lectures, hand-outs, and so on.

- Prepare a final paper that articulates the student's personal philosophy of cross-cultural counseling and his/her experience in the class. The paper is to discuss the components of the course, *their experience* taking the course, what they learned as a result of the course, how their thinking and life view changed, and how that took place. This is expected to be a thorough, thoughtful, and critical expression with a minimum of five pages. The students are encouraged to keep a personal journal during the course of such thoughts and feelings; doing so provides a great deal of material for this paper and makes the assignment less cumbersome.

- There is an attendance policy for all of the educational counseling courses at this university. Students are expected to come to class on time and prepared for the class activity. Students are also expected to participate fully in all class discussions, demonstrations, and group work. Due to the high degree of experiential instruction in the program, it is vital for the students to engage fully in the learning process.

The textbooks used for the course change periodically. Since this instructor wanted to emphasize notions of critical postmodernism, the textbooks were *Understanding Race, Ethnicity, and Power,* by E. Pinderhughes (1989) and *A Handbook for Developing Multicultural Awareness* (2nd ed.), by P. Pederson (1994). In addition to these texts, the students were provided with 11 supplemental readings. The topics of these readings ranged from bi-cultural socialization, white and male privilege, the white ethnic experience in America, the nature of prejudice and implications for counseling, and cross-cultural awareness development.

Class activities included a balance among lecture, small group activity, small group discussion, and group presentations. As with the introduction to counseling course described in Chapter 7, similar class guidelines were established and a similar classroom climate was created. There were 40 students in this class, which is large compared to past enrollment numbers for the course. Not all of the students taking the course were counseling students; there were also graduate students from educational administration, rehabilitation counseling, special education, and teacher education. This diversity proved to add a richness to the class personality as well as to the debates and discussions.

SALIENT CONCEPTS, TERMS, AND ACTIVITIES

Starting with the first class session, the students were told that their current perceptions about life and others may well be challenged in this class. This challenge is often difficult, painful, and uncomfortable. Some were expected to resist, and that was okay. Some were expected to become angry, and that was okay. Some even were expected drop out of the course, and that was okay. However, the instructor did ask that if anyone decided to drop, they first should come and talk to him/her about it. The instructor also disclosed how difficult some of these issues were with which he/she had to deal. The instructor also spoke, quite passionately, about the rewards for those who stay with the discomfort. The effort is well worth the gain of becoming a competent counselor.

Each week the instructor gave a very short lecture that reviewed the assigned reading material with a critical postmodern accent. This was introduced as a challenge of some of the more traditional theory. The students were reminded to keep open minds and to question the readings, instructor, educational systems, counseling approaches, and each other. Some of the concepts that were given extra emphasis and questioned were the definitions of culture, race, and ethnicity; dominant culture; bi-culturalism; the power in the notions of "melting pot," politically correct behaviors, "blaming the victim," and pluralism; oppression; cultural invasion; hegemony; marginality; lived experiences and contradictions; issues relating to power; and internalized racism and other "isms."

In order to facilitate engagement with the subject matter, the students participated in several small group discussions. These groups were generally four to five in membership. The students were given prepared discussion questions. The following are some examples:

- WHITE/MALE/HETEROSEXUAL PRIVILEGE—Within your small group, discuss your thoughts, feelings, opinions, and reactions to the reading about privilege. Can you think of additional unearned privileges? How does this relate to your life?

- DOMINANT CULTURE—In your group, create a list of what you believe to be the white middle-class values, beliefs, norms, customs, behaviors, and expectations. Select a spokesperson to report your group's findings.

- UNDERSTANDING POWER—Within your small group, discuss the following: (a) Share a time in your life in which you experienced power and a time in your life when you lacked power. What was the situation? What were the emotion(s) involved? (b) What are your power needs? (c) Discuss the nature of power that is inherent in the counselor–client relationship, (d) How are/will your power needs (be) fulfilled by the role of counselor? (e) What can be done in a therapeutic setting which could foster *power sharing*? Have a member of your group take summary notes to report to the class.

- YOUR IDENTITY DEVELOPMENT STAGE—Within your group, review the models of identity development (white, black, gay/lesbian, Asian, Chicano, and minority). Have each person in the group share which model and stage they most identify with at this point in their life, and why. Each person is to write on a piece of paper what they shared (model and stage) and turn it in (without names). This will serve as a survey of the class; the results will be provided next week.

• RITES OF PASSAGE—On a piece of paper, create a diagram of your life, from birth to present. This can be done in a circle formation or a straight line. Consider traditions, events, ceremonies, geographic and cultural experiences. Plot these on your diagram. Share this with your group. Allow others to ask you questions and explore the significance of this assignment.

These small group discussions created feelings of trust and intimacy in such a large class. The students were able to share their lived experiences and, for the most part, have their cultural and personal histories validated. The level of full engagement was high, which lead to "shifts" in life views, as will be discussed later.

PROFESSIONAL PRESENTATIONS

As was outlined in the course requirements, the students formed small groups to prepare and present cultural group presentations or workshops. These proved to be a culmination of research, class activities, reading, team efforts, and personal growth. Each presentation contained some element of multimedia, including video, audio, and computer. The resource packets included a wide range of information, referral options, and bibliography. What truly captured the class was the emotional commitment that each student had developed and communicated. All were emotionally and intellectually moved to new places of acceptance, compassion, and honor. It was through these final class assignments that personal growth became evident. These students became border crossers, engaging in a more complete relevancy of multicultural counseling knowledge.

Although at the graduate level one assumes and expects the students to put forth exceptional intellectual energies, these presentations far surpassed all expectations. When analyzing these outcomes, one must consider the complex constellation of instructional and personal factors at work. These include the "personhood" of the instructor, the instructor's comfort level with discomfort in the classroom, the classroom climate, the ability of all to engage in challenging subjects and move past the obstacles, and maintaining classroom guidelines. Of most importance here was a critical postmodern approach, such as fluidity, challenging norms, inclusionary efforts, mutual dialogues of respect, multiple identities, and equality. As an effort to investigate possible outcomes of this approach, the instructor decided to do a six-month follow-up with several students in the class.

Follow-up Activity

A follow-up activity was created as a way of assessing, through student responses, possible differences between a more overt approach to teaching a postmodern philosophy of counseling (Twenty-First Century Project, Chapter 7) to a more tenuous presentation. Of additional interest was any continuing effects of the course material and potential shifts in personal life views.

During the fall quarter of 1994, several of the students who completed the multicultural counseling course were asked to record on an audiotape their responses to the following six questions:

1. If true for you, in what ways did the experience of taking this course change your understanding of the multiplicity of differences found in our society?

2. Did this course change the ways in which you question and frame (define) your world? If so, how, and to what degree?

3. In what ways and how do you think this course better prepared you to deal with the challenges of being a counselor in the twenty-first century?

4. Were any of your personal concepts, beliefs, or life views challenged as a result of this experiences? If so, which concepts, beliefs, or life views? How were they challenged? What were the feelings surrounding this? And to what extent did changes occur?

5. Did this course change any perceptions that you previously held about counseling? If so, what perceptions, and how were they changed?

6. If you had to name ONE MAJOR concept, idea, or personal growth issue that resulted for you as a result of this course, discuss what that might be.

The students were asked to complete a short demographic information sheet, sign an informed consent form, take an audiotape that was provided, and at their leisure tape record their responses and return to the instructor the forms and tape in a provided self-addressed, stamped envelope. Of the 40 students who completed the class, nine were requested to complete the follow-up. Of these nine students, six mailed back the tapes, of which five were usable (one student claimed not to have the free time needed to complete the activity). The respondent pool consisted of two females and three males with an age range of 26 to 48 and a mean age of 36.5 years. Two were single, two were married, and one was divorced. The ethnic composition of the respondents was one Latina, one Jewish, one Southern African American, one African American, and one white. Their religious affiliations were one Jewish, two Christians, one Baptist, and one with no response.

STUDENT VOICES

Even though the response was slight, the comments made by these students were supportive of a critical postmodern theoretical approach and the lasting effects of this kind of educational experience. One must keep in mind that six months had passed (June to December) since these students had attended the class.

The main themes that emerged from the responses were: changes in personal understandings about multiculturalism; shifts in the framing of questions that define their realties; and changes in the perceptions held about counseling. The following student "voices" support these themes:

Changes in personal understandings about multiculturalism:

> *36-year-old white female:* Before this class, I had a "melting pot" attitude--they came from difference, but wanted to melt into the same ideals I had as a white middle-class American. I thought everyone wanted to obtain these values. I didn't see that cultural values and cultural background were important to them, and that those values were not necessarily replaced by middle-class culture.

> *30-year-old African American male:* I didn't realize how much I didn't know about multicultural [issues] until I took the course. I grew up in a small town with a population of black and white. I used to believe that the only group considered to be minorities was blacks. But now that I have been exposed to others that have experienced some of the same things that my culture has, I can relate and begin to understand.

> *26-year-old white male:* For a long time I thought that there was really no difference among people. Now I know that there is.

Shifts in framing of questions:

I'm much less judgmental in why people cannot just break loose from their family and do what is best for themselves. Now I question where they are coming from; is their background interdependent cultural beliefs as opposed to independent cultural beliefs?

Instead of measuring everyone to my yardstick of values and beliefs. . . . my values were portrayed on TV, in movies, newspapers, and magazines [and this] helped me to believe that they were universal, correct—those values of independence were the norms.

Before I took this class, I believed that every white American looked upon themselves as a member of the dominant culture. I learned that this is not true. I was surprised that some white Americans were unaware of this concept until now.

This class challenged my feelings. A light bulb went on. I was judging people from my point of view only!

My feelings of guilt from being privileged white middle-class American came to the surface in this class. I had never really admitted to myself that I was guilty about my role in society. The night I shared this in my small group, well, no one understood me. I drove home crying. Later, when we learned about the White Identity Model, I had a sigh of relief. I was able to see where I had been stuck for 20 years, and this enabled me to move on.

I believe that the change that happened to me was a process that happened to the entire class, as I was provided with new concepts, beliefs, and challenges. A process that happened from the very beginning and continued all the way through and past the end of class and is still continuing today.

Perceptions about counseling:

My old perceptions about counseling were naive. I thought that if I cared enough about the person, then that was enough. If you are not working to get into [the client's] frame of reference and understand their lived experience, you won't be effective, no matter how much you care.

The topics covered in this class have given me a framework for understanding and relating to others.

The most important thing I learned was the importance of awareness. The client's lived experience is always different than the counselor's.

Unintentional racism occurs in counseling, even among the most well-intended people. This opened my eyes tremendously—I could make [racist] assumptions too, and I need to be careful not to do that.

Because I have changed the way I look at things and define behavior, I am less likely to be frustrated when someone fails to do what I think they should do—less likely to force them or control them to make a decision which I think is right. [This is] a major issue for me as a counselor—that I don't have expectations which come from my cultural values that I am projecting onto everyone.

From the limited number of students participating in this follow-up activity, it would be hard to surmise that all of the students had similar experiences with this type of instruction. A more thorough follow-up would need to be conducted for more conclusive data. Still, these remarks are extremely encouraging and supportive. Six months after the class, these students were able to state clearly and describe shifts in the ways that they define and interpret difference.

A possible conclusion that can be drawn is that when a critical postmodern theoretical position is taken, even in this more subtle form, counseling students benefit. Although not asked, one student commented about the less direct approach,

You were actually introducing the agenda without anyone actually knowing it. It was not intrusive—not jammed down our throats. It was nice to get other points [of view] without feeling right or wrong.

Perhaps what is needed for social and personal justice is the "space to be," without feeling right or wrong. This book is not intended to declare the *right* way to educate counselors, nor is the current practice the *wrong* way. I have attempted to offer change and choice, as well as the celebration of student voice.

Bibliography

Abramowitz, S. I., & Murray, J. (1983). Race effects in psychotherapy. In J. Murray & P. R. Abramson (Eds.), *Bias in psychotherapy* (pp. 215–255). New York: Praeger.

Albee, G. W. (1981). Politics, power, prevention, and social change. In J. M. Joffe & G. W. Albee (Eds.), *Prevention through political action and social change* (pp. 3–24). Hanover, NH: University Press of New England.

Althen, G. (Ed.). (1981). *Learning across cultures.* Washington, DC: National Association for Foreign Student Affairs.

American Psychiatric Association. (1994). *Diagnostic and statistical manual of mental disorders* (4th ed., rev.). Washington, DC: American Psychiatric Association.

American Psychological Association. (1975). Report on the task force on sex bias and sex-role stereotyping in psychotherapeutic practice. *American Psychologist, 30,* 1170–1178.

American School Counselor Association. (1990). *The roles and competencies of a school counselor.* Alexandria, VA: American School Counselor Association.

Anzaldua, G. (1987). *Borderlands, La frontera.* San Francisco: Spinsters/Aunt Lute.

Aronowitz, S., & Giroux, H. A. (1991). *Postmodern education: Politics, culture, and social criticism.* Minneapolis, MN: University of Minnesota Press.

Atkinson, D. R., Morten, G., & Sue, D. W. (1983). *Counseling American minorities: A crosscultural perspective.* Dubuque, IA: Brown.

Atkinson, D. R., Morten, G., & Sue, D. W. (1989). *Counseling American minorities* (2nd ed.). Dubuque, IA: Brown.

Baritz, L. (1960). *The servants of power: A history of the use of the social sciences in American industry.* Middletown, CT: Wesleyan University Press.

Baruth, L. G., & Robinson, E. H. (1987). *An introduction to the counseling profession.* Englewood Cliffs, NJ: Prentice-Hall.

Bates, T. (1975). Gramsci and the theory of hegemony. *Journal of the History of Ideas. 36,* 351–366.

Beale, A. V. (1986). A cross-cultural dyadic encounter. *Journal of Multicultural Counseling and Development, 14,* 73–76.

Belenkey, M. J., Clinchy, B. M., Goldberger, N. R., & Tarule, J. M. (1986). *Women's ways of knowing*. New York: Basic Books.

Blocher, D. (1974). *Developmental counseling* (2nd ed.). New York: Ronald Press.

Bourdieu, P. (1979). Symbolic power. *Critique of Anthropology, 4,* 77–85.

Bowles, S., & Gintis, H. (1977). *Schooling in capitalist America*. New York: Basic Books.

Brenner, H. (1976). *Estimating the social costs of national economic policy: Implication for mental and physical and criminal aggression*. Washington, DC: U.S. Government Printing Office.

Bridges, W. (1980). *Transitions: Making sense of life's changes*. NY: Addison–Wesley.

Brown, D., & Minor, C. (1990). *Working in America: A status report on planning and problems*. Alexandria, VA: American Association for Counseling and Development.

Byrne, R. H. (1995). *Becoming a master counselor*. Pacific Grove, CA: Brooks/Cole.

California State Department of Education. (1991). *Pupil Personnel Services, school counseling specialization*. Sacramento, CA: California Teachers Credentialing Commission.

California State University, San Bernardino. (1994). *1994–1995 Bulletin, 24*(1), 6–12.

Campell, D. (1975). On the conflicts between biological and social revolution and between psychology and moral tradition. *American Psychology, 30,* 1103–1126.

Carey, J. C., Reinat, M., & Fontes, L. (1990). School counselors' perceptions of training needs in multicultural counseling. *Counselor Education and Supervision, 29,* 155–170.

Casas, J. M. (1985). A reflection on the status of racial/ethnic minority research. *The Counseling Psychologist, 13*(3), 581–598.

Chein, I. (1972). *The science of behavior and the image of man*. New York: Basic Books.

Cook, E. P. (Ed.). (1992). *Women, relationships, and power: Implications for counseling*. Alexandria, VA: American Counseling Association.

Cornforth, M. (1971). *Materialism and the dialectical method*. New York: International Publishers.

Counsel for Accreditation of Counseling and Related Educational Programs. (1993). *CACREP accreditation standards and procedures manual*. Alexandria, VA.

Dana, R. H. (1993). *Multicultural assessment persepectives for professional psychology*. Boston: Allyn & Bacon.

D'Andrea, M., & Daniels, J. (1991). Exploring the different levels of multicultural counseling training in counselor education. *Journal of Counseling and Development, 70,* 78–85.

Dant, T. (1991). *Knowledge, ideology and discourse: A sociological perspective*. London: Routledge.

Darder, A. (1991). *Culture and power in the classroom: A critical foundation for bicultural education*. New York: Bergin & Garvey.

De Boer, T. (1983). *Foundations of critical psychology*. Pittsburg: Duquesne University Press.

Dewey, J. (1966). *Democracy and education*. New York: Free Press.

Doherty, M. A. (1973). Sexual biases in personality theory. *The Counseling Psychologist, 4*, 67–74.

Doherty, W. J. (1991). Family therapy goes postmodern. *The Family Therapy Networker, 15*(5), 37–42.

Enns, C. Z. (1993). Twenty years of feminist counseling and therapy: From naming biases to implementing multifaceted practice. *The Counseling Psychologist, 21*(1), 3–87.

Facundo, A., Nuttall, E. V., & Walton, J. (1994). Culturally sensitive assessment in schools. In P. Pederson & J. C. Carey (Eds.), *Multicultural counseling in schools* (pp. 207–224). Needham Heights, MA: Allyn & Bacon.

Fay, B. (1987). *Critical social science.* Ithaca, NY: Cornell University Press.

Feinberg, W., & Soltis, J. F. (1992). *School and society.* New York: Teachers College Press.

Fernando, S. (1988). *Race and culture in psychiatry.* New York: Travistock/Routledge.

Fernando, S. (1991). *Mental health, race, and culture.* New York: St. Martin's Press.

Fine, M. (1982). *Examining inequity: View from urban schools.* University of Pennsylvania, Unpublished manuscript.

Foucault, M. (1980). *Power/knowledge: Selected interviews & other writings 1972–1977.* New York: Pantheon Books.

Fowler, J. W. (1974). Faith, liberation, and human development. *In The Foundation.* Atlanta: Grammon Theological Seminary.

Freire, P. (1970). *Pedagogy of the oppressed.* New York: Continuum.

Freire, P. (1985). *The politics of education.* New York: Bergin & Garvey.

Fukuyama, M. A. (1990). Taking a universal approach to multicultural counseling. *Counselor Education and Supervision, 30*, 6–17.

Geertz, C. (1973). *The interpretation of culture.* New York: Basic Books.

Gergen, K. J. (1991a). *The saturated self: Dilemmas of identity in contemporary life.* New York: Basic Books.

Gergen, K. J. (1991b). The saturated family. *The Family Therapy Networker, 15*(5), 27–35.

Gilbert, L. A. (1980). Feminist therapy. In A. N. Brodsky & R. T. Hare-Mustin (Eds.), *Women and psychotherapy: An assessment of research and practice.* New York: Guilford.

Giroux, H. A. (1981). *Ideology, culture, and the process of schooling.* Philadelphia: Temple University Press.

Giroux, H. A. (1983). Theories of reproduction and resistance in the new sociology of education: A critical analysis. *Harvard Educational Review, 53*, 257–294.

Giroux, H. A. (1988a). Border pedagogy in the age of postmodernism. *Journal of Education, 170*(1), 162–181.

Giroux, H. A. (1988b). *Schooling and the struggle for public life.* Minneapolis: University of Minnesota Press.

Giroux, H. A. (1992). *Border crossings: Cultural workers and the politics of education.* New York: Routledge.

Good, G. E., Gilbert, L. A., & Scher, M. (1990). Gender aware therapy: A synthesis of feminist therapy and knowledge about gender. *Journal of Counseling and Development, 68*, 376–380.

Gould, C. C. (1976). Philosophy of liberation and the liberation of philosophy. In C. C. Gould & M. W. Wartofsky (Eds.), *Women and philosophy: Toward a theory of liberation.* New York: Putnam.

Gramsci, A. (1971). *Selections from prision notebooks.* New York: International Publications.

Greenspan, M. (1983). *A new approach to women and therapy.* New York: McGraw-Hill.

Guralnik, D. B. (Ed.). (1976). *Webster's new world dictionary.* Cleveland, OH: William Collins & World Publishing Co., Inc.

Habermas, J. (1972). *Knowledge and human interests.* Boston: Beacon.

Habermas, J. (1974). *Theory and practice.* Boston: Beacon.

Hawks, B. K., & Muha, D. (1991). Facilitating the career development of minorities: Doing it differently this time. *The Career Development Quarterly, 39,* 251–260.

Heath, A. E., Neimeyer, G. J., & Frey. (1988). The future of cross-cultural counseling: A Delphi poll. *Journal of Counseling and Development, 67,* 27–30.

Held, D. (1980). *Introduction to critical theory.* Berkeley, CA: University of California Press.

Henderson, G. (1979). *Understanding and counseling ethnic minorities.* Springfield, IL: Thomas.

Hollis, J. W., & Wantz, R. A. (1993). *Counselor preparation, Volume I: Programs and personnel.* Muncie, IN: Accelerated Development Inc.

Holzkamp, K. (1976). *Grundlagen der psychologischen motivationsforsching 2.* Franfurt: Campus.

Horner, M. (1972). The motive to avoid success and changing aspirations of college women. In J. Bardwick (Ed.), *Readings on the psychology of women.* New York: Harper & Row.

Hudson, L. (1972). *The cult of the fact.* London: Jonathan Cape.

Hull, C. (1943). *Principles of behavior.* New York: Appleton Century Crofts.

Ibrahim, F. A., & Thompson, D. L. (1982). Preparation of secondary school counselors: A national survey. *Counselor Education and Supervision, 22,* 113–122.

Ivey, A. E., Ivey, M. B., & Simek-Morgan, L. (1993). *Counseling and psychotherapy: A multicultural perspective.* Needham Heights, MA: Allyn & Bacon.

Jackson, B. (1975). Black identity development: MEFORUM. *Journal of Educational Diversity and Innovation, 2,* 19–25.

Jacoby, R. (1975). *Social amnesia.* Boston: Beacon.

Jones, J., & Wilson, W. (1987). *An incomplete education.* New York: Ballantine Books.

Josselson, R. (1987). *Finding herself: Pathways to identity development in women.* San Francisco: Jossey-Bass.

Katz, J. H. (1985). The sociopolitical nature of counseling. *The Counseling Psychologist, 13*(4), 615–624.

Kellner, D. (1988). Reading images critically: Toward a postmodern pedagogy. *Journal of Education, 170*(3), 31–52.

Kelly, G. (1955). *The psychology of personal constructs.* New York: Norton.

Kohlberg, L. (1981). *The philosophy of moral development.* San Francisco: Harper & Row.

Kuhn, T. S. (1962). *The structure of scientific revolutions.* Chicago: University of Chicago Press.

Laing, R. D. (1972). The obvious. In H. M. Ruitenbeek (Ed.), *Going crazy: The radical therapy of R. D. Laing and others.* New York: Bantam Books.

Lash, S., & Urry, J. (1987). *The end of organized captitalism.* Madison: University of Wisconsin Press.

Lee, C. C., & Richardson, B. L. (Eds.). (1991). *Multicultural issues in counseling: New approaches to diversity.* Alexandria, VA: American Association for Counseling and Development.

Lee, S., & Temerlin, M. K. (1968). *Social class status and mental illness.* Unpublished doctoral dissertation, University of Oklahoma, Norman, OK.

LeVine, E. S., & Padilla, A. M. (1980). *Crossing cultures in therapy.* Monterey, CA: Brooks/Cole.

Lloyd, A. P. (1987). Multicultural counseling: Does it belong in a counselor ᵼ ̣cation program? *Counselor Education and Supervision, 26,* 164–167.

Locke, D. C. (1990). A not so provincial view of multicultural counseling. *Counselor Education and Supervision, 30,* 18–25.

Lyotard, J. (1984). *The postmodern condition.* Minneapolis: University of Minnesota Press.

MacMurray, J. (1957). *The self as agent.* London: Faber & Faber.

MacMurray, J. (1961). *Persons in relation.* London: Faber & Faber.

Margolis, R. L., & Rungta, S. A. (1986). Training counselors for working with special populations: A second look. *Journal of Counseling and Development, 64,* 642–644.

McLaren, P. (1988). Schooling the postmodern body: Critical pedagogy and the politics of enfleshment. *Journal of Education, 170,* 53–83.

McLaren, P. (1989). *Life in schools: An introduction to critical pedagogy in the foundations of education.* New York: Longman.

McLaughlin, D., & Tierney, W. G. (1993). *Naming silenced lives.* New York: Routledge.

McRae, M. B., & Johnson, S. D. (1991). Toward training for competence in multicultural counselor education. *Journal of Counseling and Development, 70,* 131–135.

Midgette, T. E., & Meggert, S. S. (1991). Multicultural counseling instruction: A challenge for faculties in the 21st century. *Journal of Counseling and Development, 70,* 136–141.

Miller, J. B. (1976). *Toward a new psychology of women.* Boston: Beacon.

Mouffe, C. (1990). Radical democracy or liberal democracy? *Socialist Review, 2,* 57–66.

Nugent, F. A. (1994). *An introduction to the profession of counseling.* New York: Macmillan College Publishing.

Nwachuku, U. T., & Ivey, A. E. (1991). Culture-specific counseling: An alternative training model. *Journal of Counseling and Development, 70,* 106–111.

O'Hara, M., & Anderson, W. T. (1991). Welcome to the postmodern world. *The Family Therapy Networker, 15*(5), 19–25.

Parham, T. (1990). *Do the right thing: Towards racial harmony in counseling psychology research.* Paper presented at the American Psychological Convention, Boston, MA, August.

Parker, W. M., Bingham, R. P., & Fukuyama, M. (1985). Improving cross-cultural effectiveness of counselor trainees. *Counselor Education and Supervision, 24,* 349–352.

Pedersen, P. (1987). Ten frequent assumptions: Cultural biases in counseling. *Journal of Multicultural Counseling and Development, 15,* 16–24.

Pedersen, P. (1988). *A handbook for developing multicultural awareness.* Alexandria, VA: American Association for Counseling and Development.

Pedersen, P. (1990). The multicultural perspective as a fourth force in counseling. *Journal of Mental Health Counseling, 12(1),* 93–95.

Pedersen, P. (1991). Multiculturalism as a generic approach to counseling. *Journal of Counseling and Development, 70,* 6–12.

Pedersen, P. (1994). *A handbook for developing multicultural awareness* (2nd ed.). Alexandria, VA: American Counseling Association.

Pedersen, P., & Carey, J. C. (1994). *Multicultural counseling in schools.* Needham Heights, MA: Allyn & Bacon.

Pedersen, P. B., Draguns, J. G., Lonner, W. J., & Trimble, J. (Eds.). (1981). *Counseling across cultures.* Honolulu: University Press.

Pinderhughes, E. (1989). *Understanding race, ethnicity, and power: The key to efficacy in clinical practice.* New York: Free Press.

Pirsig, R. M. (1974). *Zen and the art of motorcycle maintenance,* New York: Bantam Books.

Ponterotto, J. G., & Casas, J. M. (1987). In search of multicultural competence within counselor education programs. *Journal of Counseling and Development, 65,* 430–434.

Reilly, K. C. (1994). *Educational Counseling Program, program document.* Unpublished manuscript, California State University, San Bernardino, Educational Counseling Program.

Ritchie, M. H. (1994). Cultural and gender biases in definitions of mental and emotional health and illness. *Counselor Education and Supervision, 33,* 344–348.

Rodgers, R. F. (1984). Theories of adult development: Research, status, and counseling implications. In A. D. Brown & R. W. Lent (Eds.), *Handbook of counseling psychology* (pp. 479–519). New York: John Wiley & Sons.

Rogers, C. R. (1951). *Client-centered therapy.* Boston: Houghton Mifflin.

Ryan, J. (1974). Early language development: Towards a communicational analysis. In M. F. M. Richards (Ed.), *The integration of a child into a social world.* London: Cambridge University Press.

Sampson, E. (1977). Psychology and the American ideal. *Journal of Personality and Social Psychology, 35,* 767–782.

Sampson, E. (1981). Cognitive psychology as ideology. *American Psychologist, 36,* 730–743.

Sarason, S. B. (1981). *Psychology misdirected.* New York: Vintage Books.

Schlossberg, N. K. (1989). *Overwhelmed, coping with life's ups and downs.* New York: Dell Publishing.

Schultz, D. P. (1986). *Theories of personality.* Monterey, CA: Brooks/Cole.

Segall, M. H., Dansan, P. R., Berry, J. W., & Poortinga, Y. H. (1990). *Human behavior in global perspective: An introduction to cross-cultural psychology.* New York: Pergamon.

Shotter, J. (1975). *Images of man in psychological research.* London: Methuen.

Simon, R. (1987). Empowerment as a pedagogy of possibility. *Language Arts, 64,* 370–389.

Smith, E. M. J. (1985). Ethnic minorities: Life stress, social support, and mental health issues. *The Counseling Psychologist, 13,* 537–579.

Special Populations Task force of the President's Commission on Mental Health. (1978). *Task panel reports submitted to the President's Commission on Mental Health: Vol. 3.* Washington, DC: U.S. Government Printing Office.

Sue, D. W. (1973). Ethnic identity: The impact of two cultures on the psychological development of Asians in America. In S. Sue & N. N. Wagner (Eds.), *Asian Americans: Psychological perspectives* (pp. 178–206). Palo Alto, CA: Science & Behavior Books.

Sue, D. W. (1981). *Counseling the culturally different: Theory and practice.* New York: John Wiley & Sons.

Sue, D. W., & Sue, D. (1990). *Counseling the culturally different: Theory and practice.* New York: John Wiley & Sons.

Sue, D. W., Bernier, J., Durran, A., Feinberg, L., Pedsersen, P., Smith, E., & Vasquez-Nuttall, E. (1982). Position Paper: Cross-cultural counseling competencies. *The Counseling Psychologist, 10,* 45–52.

Sullivan, E. V. (1984). *A critical psychology: Interpretation of the personal world.* New York: Plenum Press.

Sullivan, E. V. (1990). *Critical psychology and pedagogy.* New York: Bergin & Garvey.

Tierney, W. G. (1993). Self and identity in a postmodern world: A life story. In D. McLaughlin & W. G. Tierney (Eds.), *Naming silenced lives: Personal narratives and processes of educational change* (pp. 119–134). New York: Routledge.

Tierney, W. G. (1995). *Building communities of difference.* Westport, CT: Bergin & Garvey.

Tolman, C. W., & Maiers, W. (Eds.). (1991). *Critical psychology: Contributions to a historical science of the subject.* New York: Cambridge University Press.

United States Bureau of the Census. (1990). *Statistical abstract of the United States* (110th ed.). Washington, DC: U.S. Government Printing Office.

Usher, C. H. (1989). Recognizing cultural bias in counseling theory and practice: The case of Rogers. *Journal of Multicultural Counseling and Development, 17,* 16–24.

Van Hesteren, F., & Ivey, A. E. (1990). Counseling and development: Toward a new identity for a profession in transition. *Journal of Counseling and Development, 68,* 524–528.

Van Wormer, K. (1989). Co-dependency: Implications for women and therapy. *Women and Therapy, 8*(4), 51–63.

Velsquez, R. J., Johnson, R., & Brown-Cheatham, M. (1993). Teaching counselors to use the *DSM-III-R* with ethnic minority clients: A paradigm. *Counselor Education and Supervision, 32,* 323–331.

Webster's encyclopedic unabridged dictionary of the English language. (1989). New York: Portland House.

White, J. L. (1984). *The psychology of blacks: An Afro-American perspective.* Englewood Cliffs, NJ: Prentice-Hall.

White, T. J., & Sedlacek, W. E. (1987). White students' attitudes toward Black and Hispanics: Programming implications. *Journal of Multicultural Counseling and Development, 15, 171–183.*

Wilden, A. (1975). *Structure and transformation: Developmental and historical aspects.* New York: John Wiley & Sons.

Williams, R. (1973). Base and superstructure in Marxist cultural theory. *New Left Review, 82,* 3–16.

Williams, R. (1976). *Key words: A vocabulary of culture and society.* London: Fontana Croom Helm.

Willis, P. (1983). Cultural production and theories of reproduction. In L. Barton & S. Walker (Eds.), *Race, class, and education.* London: Fontana Croom Helm.

Wrenn, C. (1962). The encapsulated counselor. *Harvard Educational Review, 32*(4), 444–449.

Wrenn, C. (1965). The culturally encapsulated counselor revisited. In P. Pederson (Ed.), *Handbook of cross-cultural counseling and therapy* (pp. 323–329). Westport, CT: Greenwood.

Yamamoto, J., James, Q. C., & Palley, N. (1968). Cultural problems in psychiatric therapy. *Archives of General Psychiatry, 19,* 45–49.

Young, R. L., Chamley, J. D., & Withers, C. (1990). Minority faculty representation and hiring practices in counselor education programs. *Counselor Education and Supervision, 29,* 148–154.

Index

About the Author

SUSAN J. BROTHERTON is Assistant Professor of the Educational Counseling Program at California State University, San Bernardino.

ISBN 0-89789-471-5

EAN

9 780897 894715

HARDCOVER BAR CODE